THE BUILT

UP SOUL

GOD IS NOT MOVED BY CHANCE

FAITH AND TRUTH

MOVES GOD

The Giving Up Of Our Self To God; I Must Die To Self That My Soul Lives Eternally

By

MARGERY JOHNSON WOLFE

Print information available on the last page.

Rev. date: 06/14/2017

THE BUILT UP SOUL

Dedication

This book is dedicated to all men, women, boys and girls that hopes to see God one day!

It is dedicated to those called, chosen, anointed and appointed to do purpose in the earth as God's Spirit filled, Spirit led and Spirit controlled leading men and women

It is my prayer for my fellow yoke men in the Gospel that we pursue Truth and build up our Faith in the Holy Ghost that will bring us to know God in a very special significant way

I humbly dedicate this book to my sons, daughters in laws, grandchildren, and great grandchildren here and to come

I dedicate it to my parents, brothers and sisters as well as all of my family inclusively

I dedicate it to my Church; my spiritual family and friends

I finally dedicate it to all that make up God's earth

THE BUILT UP SOUL

Table of Contents

THE BUILT UP SOUL

THE BUILT UP SOUL

Introduction

In life we will learn some things! From the time a child is born in this world; they are learning. We learn how that we should live life in this world. What we learn early in life has everything to do with how we will leave the earth. A child learns what they live and live what they learn.

When Adam was created in this world, he knew nothing of the world. He just roamed around in the world with Eve at his side free from the contaminants of the earth. God had made them in the earth but they knew not the world they were in. But thanks to the mean subtle demonic force; Satan they would soon like a new born baby learn some things about where they were.

They were sinless, full of light. There were no darkness in them for they were the light of the world. They were full of God. They set in a high place, a city that could not be hid for their purity illuminated the earth.

The light of the body is the eye; therefore when thine eye is single Jesus said in *Luke 11:34* thy whole body also is full of light; but when thine eye is evil, thy body also is full of darkness. When we God's created and made beings realize who we really are; we too will choose light over darkness. It was in God we had life; its still like that today.

When life as we know it is passed; we still have life in the Spirit that man was in his first state. Adam and Eve were created first spiritually, then made naturally. God's light shined through them even after they were put inside made bodies; different in nature with different functions. Samuel said in *I Samuel 20:3* truly as the Lord liveth and as thy soul liveth, there is but one step between me and death.

Because of the spiritual death Adam and Eve brought forth to man, death now both naturally and spiritually happens. Death is imminent and we know not when it

4

THE BUILT UP SOUL

will come. We are in the world but not of the world. How death finds us and our life lived determines our resting place away from earth.

The light of God that shined forth within them was replaced with emptiness and darkness; yet they comprehended it not. They knew a change came because they found themselves naked as they always was. But something happened and they knew it; but didn't know until God spoke his disapproval of their actions.

God still tell man today of our sins. Repent them and quit doing them! We are better than what the world have to offer us! Be the light with the light God sent to bring man out of darkness once again! Hear one day God say welcome home thy good and faithful servant; enter into rest.

THE BUILT UP SOUL

The Built Up Soul

Living To Live Again is what we are doing in the earth.

Psalm 49:6-9, they that trust in their wealth and boast themselves in the multitude of their riches; none of them can by any means redeem his brother, nor give to God a ransom for him; for the redemption of their soul is precious and it ceaseth forever; that he should still live forever and not see corruption.

What is the weakness in this world all about? We as the called and elect of God is built up by God through His Word by His Spirit that first gave man life; God breathed his Spirit in man and he became a living soul.

Genesis 2:7 and the Lord God formed man of the dust of the ground and breathed into his nostrils, the breath of life and man became a living soul.

Mankind today is weakened by the fact that the Holy Spirit, the power of God and the Word is not a part of man's life. We have put away from us that which matters; God's spiritual ruling part of us.

That spiritual part of man that cries for attention lies deficient every day because man refuse to nourish their soul. The soul is that spiritual nature in man which is more than what is found in the Creation. It is spiritual reasoning and immortal.

Leviticus 17:11 for the life of the flesh is in the blood and I have given it to you upon the altar to make an atonement for your souls; for it is in the blood that maketh an atonement for the soul.

THE BUILT UP SOUL

Ecclesiastes 3:21-22 who knoweth the spirit of man that goeth upward and the spirit of the beast that goeth downward to the earth? Wherefore I perceive that there is nothing better than that a man should rejoice in his own works; for that is his portion, for who shall bring him to see what shall be after him?

Matthew 10:28 and fear not them which kill the body but are not able to kill the soul: but rather fear him which is able to destroy both soul and body in hell. The word soul is synonymous with the life of man. So then we should worry about the one that gave us a soul.

Psalm 7:5-11 let the enemy persecute my soul and take it: yea let him tread down my life upon the earth and lay my honor in the dust, Selah. Arise oh Lord in thine anger, lift up thyself because of the rage of mine enemies and awake for me to the judgment, that thou has commanded. So shall the congregation of the people compass Thee about for their sakes; therefore return thou on high. The Lord shall judge the people; judge me O Lord according to my righteousness and according to my integrity that is in me. Oh let the wickedness of the wicked come to an end; but establish the just; for the righteous God trieth the hearts and reins. My defense is of God, which safety the upright in heart. God judgeth the righteous and God is angry with the wicked everyday.

We must speak to ourselves concerning our soul. I am a child of God chosen for this time. Now if any have a problem with that, talk to God about it; after all He is yet in control. I will tell you though, if you want to anger Him keep trying to match wits with Him. You are not fighting me; I am here because He allowed me to be.

Psalm 33:19 says it is God that deliver our soul from death and to keep us alive in famine. Remember it was God that hardened Pharoah's heart when Moses was trying to bring them out of Egypt. We here in America don't want God's wrath. We want to continue giving Him glory that we keep our confidence in God. I am a man but I am not God, I can only here one person speaking at a time. When you make your appointment we will talk! Let's agree to disagree!

The two main doctrines entertained by Theologians concerning the nature of man are: (1). Dichotomy, which declares that there are two essential parts in man; the body, which is material and the soul, or principal of life and (2). Trichotomy, which declares that man is made up of body, soul, and spirit (*Thessalonians 5:23*). The Bible doesn't declare for either view.

We must build to stand; therefore we must trust God and his Word individually! As we will find in the Bible, God does however teach us of man's higher spiritual nature, soul, or personality; and that this is to live on is a part of the Divine plan of God. We must hearken to and be found doing the Word.

James 1:19-23 wherefore my beloved brethren let every man be swift to hear, slow to speak, slow to wrath; for a man of wrath works not the righteousness of God. Wherefore lay apart all filthiness and superfluity of naughtiness and receive with meekness the engrafted Word which is able to save your souls. But be ye doers of the Word and not hearers only; deceiving your own selves. For if any be a hearer of the Word and not a doer, He is like unto a man beholding his natural face in a glass.

Have anyone besides me took a look in the mirror lately! If I am wrong I ask for your forgiveness; forgive me! It was never a part in my heart to hurt anyone in my challenge to call all of us to a place of accountability that God would be pleased with. We all must come to a place where we break down the folly in our lives.

My only problem is I want God to be the greater part of all of men lives again. Like me, one day at God's appointed time you are getting up our of here too! Don't allow hatred, envy, jealousy and all the likes thereof to keep us out of heaven.

Our relationship must be right with God. Tomorrow is not promised to any of us. As servants we must be submissive to God and those in authority. As believers in the Lord Jesus Christ we must be subject to every human institution. Don't let anyone or anything stand in the way of us going to heaven.

We must forgive all that have stood in protests against the advancement of God in this world. Why? Forgiveness is a vital part of man's life that brings glory to God. It's no easy task Jesus had in representing all people while we yet desired to continue in sin.

Peter said in *1 Peter 1:9* receiving the end of your faith, even the salvation of your souls. Would any of

THE BUILT UP SOUL

us want Christ to meet us on the lighted path and turn us away saying we are not worthy to be taken to the Father?

While I can only speak for me; I am not going back, I am looking forward for the prize of the higher calling in Christ. I am searching for a higher calling of Christ that has been revealed to me. I just want to take you with me. I want Him to be revealed to you that you will realize I am not trying to hurt anyone but bring order to everyone.

We take one step at a time to right every wrong in our lives, but its going to take cooperation on all of our part; mind, body, soul, spirit and body which must align itself with the Word of God. We are through God's Word built to stand in these evil times!

We are a people that was built on the foundation of God through the Word by the power of the Holy Ghost. He is here to help us to go back to being a people that trust God again and love one another no matter our ethnic background, the color of our skin, how much or how little we have.

The supreme value of the soul is declared by our Lord and Savior Jesus Christ in *Matthew 16:26* which says, for what is man profited if he shall gain the whole world and lose his own soul? Or what shall a man give in exchange for his soul? The soul is the life of man. Nothing we can obtain in this life can replace the soul.

David expressed even before Jesus came in *Psalm 49:6-9*, they that trust in their wealth and boast themselves in the multitude of their riches; none of

THE BUILT UP SOUL

them can by any means redeem his brother, nor give to God a ransom for him; for the redemption of their soul is precious and it ceaseth forever; that he should still live forever and not see corruption.

Its either one way in this life we live; either for God after His Holy and righteous Word or after Satan, the prince of the air in this world and his evil ways. Either we are governed by God and lead by His Holy Spirit or we are under the spell of evil; governed by Satan.

Either we are living for what's right or we are dying for what's wrong. When we know to do better; we are to do better. We must be examples of the Lord Jesus Christ.

In the age to come we will stand as a sign built upon the favor of God. That sign will be an outward fact that served as a pledge of God's Divine promise. God throughout the age of man have given us signs to confirm the words of the Prophets.

The angels at the birth of Jesus gave the Shepherds a sign, *Luke 2:8-12*. They told the Shepherds that this day they bring them news that would be to all people. For unto you this day in the City of David a Savior which is Christ the Lord is born. As a sign to you, you shall find Him wrapped in swaddling clothes, lying in a manger. The sign given would lead them safely to the Savior born into the world; they made haste to get there. He was found. They returned home glorifying and praising God for all the things they had heard and seen.

THE BUILT UP SOUL

God Is Not Moved By Chance

WHY would anyone wrap God up in a box? In a raffle? In an egg? God is not a God of chance! He is not a God of fortune or fate! Christians today as well of the general mockers of God celebrate Him in chocolates, Santa Claus, rabbits and eggs. That is not God but gods, idols, idolatry indeed!

Ecclesiastes 9:11-12 I returned and saw under the Sun, that the race is not to the swift, nor the battle to the strong, neither yet bread to the wise, nor yet riches to men of understanding, nor yet favor to men of skill; But time and chance happened to them all. For man also knoweth not his time: as the fishes that are taken in an evil net, and as the birds that are caught in a snare; so are the sons of men snared in an evil time, when it fallen suddenly upon them.

Luke 12:20 but God said unto Him, thou fool, this night the soul shall be required of thee; then whose shall those things be which thou has provided?

We must be careful of what we lay to the charge of God. Life is not a chance, either we have life or we don't. With God either we have Him or we don't. either our works will bring glory to Him or it don't. Blessed is the man who trust is in God. Blessed is the man who has his hope in God. Our works must be that of the Lord Jesus Christ; not our way!

Where lies the fruit of our yielding labor? Where are the souls generated from the fruit of our labor? What souls will our labor reach? The Lord searched the heart, He tries the reins even to give every man according to his ways, and according to the fruit of his doings. God test the emotions and repeats. We must be careful of what we lay to God. The heart is deceitful above all things and desperately wicked; who can know it? (*Jeremiah 17:9*)

Solomon the King found in his dealings with people that he needed wisdom, knowledge and understanding. That is he needed God, his Word and the Holy Spirit all working in his house. He had a judgment call in *1 Kings 3:16* that showed his knowledge of human nature. His interest in religion seemed to be in its outward aspects, for his work was bestowed upon that which maketh for demonstration and show.

Solomon had high ideals early in life, but was carried away from them by His desire for show and power through those things foreign to God. He loved women that was strange (foreign) and allowed them their own worship. His association with foreign nations brought idolatry into his own realm.

Solomon in this seemingly human book of Ecclesiastes mirrors the experiences of those who dwell wholly in the realm of material things and it shows how little the world can satisfy the soul of man apart from God. He tells us that He is not speculative; moral not skeptical for he holds fast his faith in God.

We too as Solomon did must find purpose to find the highest good in life. His conclusion is one; fear God and keep His Commandments. Wisdom in the technical sense of God's world plan; its his Divine Providence. The wise men in Israel *Jeremiah*

THE BUILT UP SOUL

18:18, were philosophers who cared almost nothing for the ritual of the priests and quite as little for the distinctively national ideals of the prophets.

Life was interpreted from the human point of view. How many times do we do the same? God's people leaves his Divine principles to follow that which benefit the human nature rather than the spiritual. We leave God to run after the wealth of the world instead of work the work of soul winning as Jesus set forth to us in ***Matthew 28:19-20***. God has a Way we are to take. All human efforts is without profit.

God is not a God of chance. There is nothing new under the Sun. life is a weary monotony, an endless treadmill, because man's spirit is so much larger than his sphere. All is vanity Solomon found out because man is not free. We search for the highest good in life when it's actually that which we can't see, touch, feel or comprehend that which is of the greatest importance. God's business is soul business!

After this realization Solomon concluded that we are to rejoice in God, remember God in our youth, keep His Commandments, and fear God. Man today fear not God so they take chances they should not. We find today as then man is full of wretchedness and squalor. Meaning they are a deeply distressed people, unhappy, miserable and unfortunate. They are characterized by causing others distress likewise. The saying is misery loves company. The world is full of contempt, man is despised and scorned because they have been labeled something they know not of. Much branding goes on in the world where man is neglecting the very part of Him that will build them up.

They are squalid; foul and unclean because they neglect the sanitary conditions of God for the sordid world. Man refuses wisdom for pleasure. They will receive in them things that is against God and nature for monetary wealth. Man will plunge deep into delights that they may still the burning thirst of passionate desires in their flesh; chancing God come not at that moment.

Pleasure they find only brought them pain afterwards; yet they still take chances. If God is not a part of our pleasure it is all vanity. Money every day fails to secure man happiness. No matter how much they have or don't have there is no joy without God! The competition to get it, the oppression to have it, or the foolish speculation that having wealth satisfies brings not with it; joy.

Solomon says apart from God all is vanity. Keep God in the forefront of your business. A rich man would love the opportunity to enjoy his wealth. To become popular comes with some compromise. It will bring forth death before the time. We in Christ is compromising God's love for things of the world that we be known and seen.

Whatsoever thy hand finder to do, do it with the might; for there is no work, nor device, nor knowledge, nor wisdom, in the grave, wither thou goest, (*Ecclesiastes 9:10*).

The wise man seeks out God without procrastination. We should think of God in our youth while we have strength to do that which God requires. Loving God is the real focus of man which is to be instilled in them while they are young. We cannot lack the knowledge needed to follow away from immortality; which Solomon lacked but learned.

To have all things in life but lacking in the love of God with faith and truth is vanity! Solomon considered his own life in delivering this message to us in Ecclesiastes. After really seeing God as He is presented in real life Solomon returned and saw under the Sun that the race is not to the swift, nor the battle to the strong, neither yet bread to the wise, nor yet riches to men of understanding, nor yet favor to men of skill; but time and chance happens to them all.

No man knows the time of their demise just as fishes know when they are caught up in an evil net or the birds caught in a snare. Therefore man is ensnared in an evil time, when it falls suddenly upon them. Satan tricked man up from the beginning. Adam was ensnared deceptively and man still fall to the Devil's deceptive practices.

Jesus in **Matthew 24:12-13** said because iniquity (hidden sin) shall abound, the love of many shall was cold, but he that endure to the end the same shall be saved.

Man's soul will be required of God one day. Will he take all that he has acquired in earth with him? We must rethink our position in earth. We must realize what is important. We must realize what is right and proper before God. For what is a man profited if he gain the whole world and lose his soul?

THE BUILT UP SOUL

Look at the time in which we now live. Nations are rising against nations, kingdoms against kingdoms, there are great earthquakes in divers places, there are famines and pestilences, fearful sights and great signs from heaven as Jesus said there would be; yet we chance God?

Today, let all that will hear; God is not a God of chance. Don't chance with our soul or the souls of others. Let what we have done in the world become a testimony of deliverance that man will hear the Gospel and be healed, delivered and set free.

Settle the Gospel, the Word in your hearts today, meditate upon the Lord; for He will give you a mouth and wisdom, which all of your adversaries shall not be able to gainsay nor resist. You may be betrayed by all people you may know in this world considered to be important in your life; but persevere with God even if it causes your death.

It's better to be hated of all people than to be with the hated of God for eternity.

THE BUILT UP SOUL

Faith And Truth Moves God

Faith, what is faith? Truth, what is truth? God is a God of truth. He has redeemed man and we accept his Word, that the Lord is right and all his works are done in truth. Mercy and truth are met together that produces faith in the believer once they have accepted the Truth of God. We shall know the truth and it will make us free.

Deuteronomy 32:4 all his ways are judgment, a God of truth and without iniquity; just and right is He!

Romans 1:16-17 for I am not ashamed of the Gospel of Christ, for it is the power of God unto salvation, to everyone that believeth; to the Jew first, and also to the Greek. For therein is the righteousness of God revealed from faith to faith; as it is written, the just shall live by faith.

The lip of Truth shall be established forever, but a lying tongue is but for a moment. Truth is noted in the Scripture. Jesus, the Word was made flesh and dwelt among men to bring forth the truth to man. He was full of grace and truth. It is in Him we have faith to believe in God. He is the Way, the Truth and the Life, **John 14:6**.

Paul in Romans teaches us that we are not to be shamed of the Gospel of Jesus Christ. The Gospel is the Truth of Christ! It is the manifested power of God which draws man to Him. It is the power of God unto salvation to all that believe. We are to hope in the Lord; for it is in Him we are justified freely by His grace through redemption.

THE BUILT UP SOUL

Romans is the greatest of Paul's Epistles. He states the theme for his writing to the Gentiles at Rome. He was an Apostle of Christ to the Gentiles. The Church at Rome was composed of both Jews and Gentiles. He presented them with the Gospel of grace. They had not yet heard him preach but this Epistle served as a specimen of his theology and preaching. He promoted unity between Christians.

Paul dealt more with principles and less with details but it met the demands them and now with marvelous success. He showed forth the necessity of the God kind of righteousness for the whole of man; both Jews and Gentiles which is by faith in Christ. Faith is the belief, confidence or trust we have in God. All faith is based upon testimony or evidence; NO evidence, no faith. Although we have never seen God we believe that He is and that He is a rewarder to them that diligently seek Him.

God has sent His Son into the world, the second Adam to redeem men and therefore He requires man to accept Jesus as the Christ. Jesus was as Adam was birth forth by God. He has preserved for and presented to the world through His Word sufficient evidence them that Jesus is the Christ.

Many other signs Jesus did in the presence of his disciples that they believed then and we may believe now that Jesus was the long promised Messiah; Christ. We have life through his Name, *John 20:30-31*. Faith in the Truth comes through hearing and hearing by the Word of God, *Romans 10:17*.

THE BUILT UP SOUL

Now that we have the evidence, where is our Faith? He is ur Truth presented. God has this provided the world with ample evidence to produce faith. We are required to believe that Jesus is the Christ and to submit to Him. He tells us we will be condemned if we do not receive Him as Lord; Christ, **Mark 16:16**.

Jesus said except ye believe that I am He, ye shall die in your sins. Without faith it is impossible to please God or to come to Him, **Hebrews 11:6**. Unbelievers will hear the Word and choose to accept it or not. For this reason Jesus sends us out as was the disciples sent in **Matthew 28:19-20**, go into all the world and preach the Gospel.

The Gospel is to be made known to all nations for the obedience of faith, **Romans 16:25-26**. How shall they believe in Him whom they have not heard? And how shall they hear without a preacher, **Romans 10:14**? It pleased God by the foolishness of preaching to save them that believe, **1 Corinthians 1:21**.

Faith is not only dependent upon evidence, it is conditioned by it. It partakes of the very essence of the testimony or evidence producing it. If the evidence is grotesque, fanatical or false, so will be the faith it produces. Then again the evidence is true, so will the faith it produces. The more evidence a lawyer have in a courtroom doing trial that's true, the more faith they have that they will win their case.

We have Divine Testimony of Christ; therefore we have divine faith. Like evidence, like faith. It is absolutely essential therefore that the Gospel be preached in purity.

For this cause Apostle Paul warns of false prophets and teachers who pervert the Gospel for their own purposes. He pronounced a curse upon anyone, man or Angel who preached any other Gospel than that we have preached, **Galatians 1:8-9**. It is not faith, faith in just any sort of gospel that will save, but faith in the true and unadulterated Gospel of Christ.

Salvation is not dependent upon faith but "the faith". For that reason **Jude 3** exhorts us as Christians to contend earnestly for the faith which was once for all delivered unto the Saints. We are to be glad in the Lord, trust and have our hope in Him. We are not to forget his works and keep His Commandments. The man that trust in God is blessed.

Now therefore faith and truth moves God! All his ways are judgment, a God of truth and without iniquity; just and right is He! When we are not ashamed of the Truth we confess we will walk out in the faith it has produced. We live by faith. We have peace with God through our Lord Jesus Christ because we are justified by faith.

God has filled us with his hope, joy and peace in believing, that we may abound in hope, the Lord God keep us through the power of the Holy Ghost. Catch on to faith today.

THE BUILT UP SOUL

Deceived, Dejected, Denied

Why would we say man is deceived? How did we get to the point of being deceived? Deceit is a falsehood, the tongue of man can be an instrument of deceit that purely comes from their heart. Deceit is characteristic of the heart and God abhors it.

Proverbs 11:18 the wicked worker a deceitful work; but to him that speaks righteousness shall be a sure reward.

Galatians 6:3 for if anyone thinks he is something when he is nothing, He deceive himself.

God forbids man to be deceptive; as Christ whom we mirror was perfectly free from deceit. Deceit covers a wide area of man's life in earth. We are deceived by Satan in the Garden of Eden first with Adam and Eve.

Genesis 1:27 so God created man in his own image, in the image of God created he him; male and female created he them.

Genesis 2:7 and the Lord God formed man of the dust of the ground, and breathed into his nostrils the breath of life: and man became a living soul.

God had given them all that they would need in the earth. They were not told of Satan and evil spirits; just one simple request God asked them to obey; **Genesis 2:16-17** to not eat of one tree in the midst of the Garden; the tree of the knowledge of good and evil.

Satan being more subtle than them got them in trouble with God. What we don't know can hurt us.

22

THE BUILT UP SOUL

They didn't know the consequences of not obeying but they learned real quick. Their actions birth forth a life man yet today suffer from. Satan stood as a witness against God and what He had said to them once he realized they were not aware of Him.

He used the serpent's lips to deceive them. We must be careful of what we witness and who we witness to. It could come back and bite us. Watch them that always have fair speech. Don't believe the fair words of one we know is a devil. Solomon says in **Proverbs 26:25** there are seven abominations in his heart.

Jeremiah 17:9 the heart is deceitful above all things and desperately wicked; who can know it. Let no man deceive you with vain words; for because of these things cometh the wrath of God upon the children of disobedience.

He that will love life and see good days, let him refrain his tongue from evil and his lips that he speak no guile. We are to keep our self free from deceit; avoid it, shun those that are given to deceit for it can be addicting. Pray for them that they be delivered from that spirit of deceit.

When we cross paths with one that teaches deceit, beware of them that we don't lay aside seeking truth to follow after deceit.

Dejected, What does it mean to be dejected? Are we one that has been dejected? Dejected means to be cast down in spirit, disheartened, depressed. Who is it that seek to keep us low in spirits? **Genesis 6:5-7** and God saw the that the wickedness of man was great in the earth and that every imagination of the thoughts of his heart was only evil continually and it repented the Lord that he had made man upon the earth and it grieved him at his heart. And the Lord said, I will destroy man whom I have created from the face of the earth. , we must be careful of what God sees in our lives.

Man because of their evil wicked ways and sin dejected even God. So now if the sin of man does not bother us believers, we need to go and evaluate our relationship with God again.

Denied, exactly what do we mean? It means God has said no to an act or request. It means He has rejected our gifts or offering. God has disowned what w say was done in his name. It means that God have somewhat of an ought against them that is being denied.

God had been gracious is what Ananias name meant; he tried to enhance his reputation by a show of liberality; He sold property and pretended to give the entire proceeds to the church but his deceit and its deliberate purpose was made known to him by Peter.

Peter laid bare his sin to Ananias guilty conscience and he dropped dead in shock (*Acts 5:1-11*).

Ananias was denied the blessing of God for his deceitfulness in the matter. He and his wife Sapphira had plotted to deceive the people of God.

Not knowing her husband had dropped dead at the feet of deception, she carried out her part and she too dropped dead.

THE BUILT UP SOUL

Many people still carry out this deception in churches when it comes to them bringing an offering, sacrificing their time, talents, and gifts before men. They lay half acts before man like God doesn't know what they are doing. They write out checks to the Ministry that never get deposited and cashed unbeknown to the people.

To be deceitful is a sin, a lie, a falsehood. Unbeknown to man the tongue can be an instrument of deceit. Deceit comes from the heart. Ananias and Sapphira planned and plotted this deception and carried it out. What they thought was hid from man was not hid from God.

God spoke at the mouth of Peter by the Spirit letting them know He knew. Be sure our sin will find us out. Be free of deceitfulness, don't lie and pretend to do something, don't purpose evil in our hearts. Lay aside all wickedness and don't pull others in to do wrong with you.

We don't want to be deceived, dejected and denied by God even if we are by man. In life we have a place we want to get in Christ and in the world but it must come by way of righteousness.

Righteousness will bring us to our desired end; that destined place.

What is destiny? Destiny is that predetermined course of events, fate, particular persons fate or lot, something which a person or thing is destined, the designated, assigned, dedicated place one should be that they have been directed, devised or set apart for a specific purpose or place. Predestined event may be held to be an irresistible power or agency. Predetermine means to determine or decree beforehand, fixed, prearranged, pre-established, preplanned, preset, set up Predestined determined before hand, ordain in advance by divine will or as if by fate. Destiny, doom, fate, predetermination.

Genesis 37:3-6 Now Israel (Jacob) loved Joseph more than all his children, because he was the son of his old age, and he made him a coat of many colors and when his brethren saw that their father loved him more than all his brethren they hated him and could not speak peaceably unto him and Joseph dreamed a dream, and he told it his brethren and they hated him yet the more, and he said unto them, hear I pray you, this dream which I have dreamed.

In the text we find that Joseph was the son of Jacob and his beloved wife Rachel. He was hated for his dreams, his passions, and his purpose, as well as the favoritism his father showed him over his other brothers; for whom he was the eleventh of the twelve sons and the eldest of the two children of Rachel and Jacob.

Jacob was around 90-91 years of age when Joseph was born, so he was his favorite son because his birth was in his advanced years and born of the woman he truly loved that had been barren. Joseph received a coat of many colors from his father and this excited envy among the other brethren.

His brothers then conspired against him, sold him to the Ishmaelite, and they sold him into Egypt, but the Lord was with Joseph and as *Jeremiah*

THE BUILT UP SOUL

29:11 says, for I know the thoughts that I think toward you, saith the Lord, thoughts of peace and not of evil, to give you an expected end.

He was delayed but not denied God's destiny for his life because Joseph had God's favor, he also found favor with man. He found grace in the King's sight. He served the King and the King made him overseer over his house and all that he had.

Knowing your destiny will keep you focused and from falling into temptation along the way, although the Devil will set traps for you. Ananias and Sapphira didn't realize the trap Satan set for them.

He will set out deception, he will even have us incarcerated; bound up in our mind that our destiny will be cut short, but little did he know that all things work together for good to them that Love God and is called according to his purpose. Joseph purpose was fulfilled in his gift in the jail. His gift made room for him.

His gift of interpretation got him out of jail, in second command only to the king. He interpreted the Kings dream. The same gift that got him bound up in life also got him freed to save his people as well as the nation of Egypt. He ended up getting his father and family back, kept them from starvation as well as Egypt.

Because he stayed the course, he not only saved them but he showed the love of God and that God was in control of his destiny and his life. He lived out his God ordained purpose to meet his destiny, his desired end no matter the opposition and deceit he faced. Joseph's destiny came to pass because he was careful about where he went and what he did when he got there. No matter what happened in his life, he did not become rebellious, but stayed true to God and kept God first.

He was given to ethics in his work, he had a moral mandate for his work in whatever state that he found himself in. He did the right things, lived a certain way (Godly), carried himself like he had purpose, what he did was of a good report although it was reported wrong and he dealt with things in a godly fashion never deviating away from his divine destiny. He ran from the things of the flesh and to the things of Christ.

Although we may have been delayed some things in life, keep living. Live for God, stay in the race, and forgive when needed and run for your life away from sin, and fulfill your destiny. In reaching our desired end or our destiny you must shut in with the lover of your soul.

Destiny brings life to dead situations; it brings hope to hopeless lives. To stay pure, stay in the Word, stay with the Word, and go back to our first state, purity, cleanliness, and sanctification. That first state where Jesus was in total control.

THE BUILT UP SOUL

What's Our Profession

Romans 1:22 Professing themselves to be wise they become fools

Professing is declaring or admitting openly or freely in words or appearance or confessing something known or believed to be a fact.

Wise means characterized by wisdom, marked by deep understanding, keen discernment and a capacity for sound judgment, prudent, knowing, crafty, shrewd, insolent, or smart-alecky.

What makes man think that they can run from the presence of God when he is omnipotent? He is everywhere at all times and is in every place at the same time. Adam and Eve after they had disobeyed God and sinned in the Garden tried to run from his presence. Why, because they were ashamed. Guilt says I did wrong, shame says I am wrong.

These people are only wise in their own conceit. They want people to see and think that they are sound in their judgment and have great understanding of people and situations, unusual discernment and judgment in dealing with them. They also suggest that they wide experience, great learning and wisdom great sagacity and discernment stresses that they have a great capacity for reaching wise decisions or conclusions.

They are usually the ones that exercise the most restraint of sound practical wisdom and discretion, their actions are guided and restrained by good sense and rationality and mental soundness, rationality and level headedness remains the same; even in crises. A wise man however is one of unusual learning, judgment, or insight, versed in esoteric love and wit.

THE BUILT UP SOUL

They come to know, learn knowledge, has reasoning power, intelligent, resourceful, astuteness of perception or judgment, has the ability to relate seemingly disparate things, clever or apt humor, person of superior intellect, a thinker, a power to evoke laughter and can expose or ridicule conduct doctrines or institutions either by direct criticism, writing, or more often through irony.

The wise man has an ability also to answer quickly, pointedly or wittily using wisdom, knowing when, where, how, why, and who of a matter. They must discern when to speak, know what to say, how to say it, know why it must be said and who to say it to and in front of who else.

Now the problem starts or begins when this wisdom is used in the wrong context and the wise person goes against the ordinances of God. The wisdom a man possesses comes from God and God's trust them with it. All of Gods works are manifest through wisdom he has given man.

Wisdom and might belongs only to God and it is he that gives wisdom and knowledge to them that know understanding. In the misuse of this wisdom principalities and powers in the earth are opened up in the lives of others. The wisdom that God meant to be manifested to the church and known by the church has been removed.

Therefore because of what a person thought made them foolish in the sight of God soon made them steal God's glory, blessings, wisdom, thanksgiving, honor, power and might that only God should receive from a man in the earth. Sin enters in the form of pride and they promise that they can take a person to the promise land outside of God. They deviate from the acceptable standard and become an idol. Instead of people following God they follow the man, worshipping him as that idol and sin conceived individually. They are thought to be wise, but they are fools.

A fool is one destitute of understanding, reason or moral sense. Fools deny God and they make mock at sin, despise instruction, pours folly out of their mouths, and they love simplicity. A fool loves living on the edge and mischief is bound in their hearts. They think that they must tell all for they are full of words, utters their mind, are hasty in spirit to be angry; for anger rests in the bosom of fools.

Proverbs 18:6-7, a fool's lips enter into contention and his mouth calleth for strokes. A fool's mouth is his destruction and his lips are the snare of his soul.

Fools are full of pride and glory in his wisdom, might, and riches. Their thoughts are that they are wise but it is the Lord that exercises loving kindness, judgment, and righteousness in the earth. There is a generation that is pure in their eyes, and yet is not washed from their filthiness.

Their foolish pride will not allow them to realize the error of their ways, every one is wrong except them. Self exaltation is bliss in the mind of the fool and they usually think more highly of themselves than they ought to because they are intoxicated with vain glory.

The only thing a fool can do is realize that they need the Lord, accept Christ in their lives according to the foreknowledge of God the Father through sanctification of the Spirit unto obedience and sprinkling of the blood of Jesus Christ if they are ever to have any hope of eternal life

THE BUILT UP SOUL

The One God Called To Give Life

Man, God's perfect man, has been imperfect since right after creation with their hearts seared with disobedience. God made man a woman that he may have a more perfect life and even yet today he causes death to come to her over and over again, until ultimately the flesh takes no more and give up the ghost.

Instead of Marriage, man chooses to just have immoral sex with woman. Instead of woman saying no, she yield her self to man.

Now the world has a curse over it and we wonder why. We wonder how we arrived at that state. Let me give you the answer. Disobedience is a reproach against any nation. The world is sex crazed. They does not respect the order of God's creation in their foolishness. They are committing unnatural sins as well as the natural sin.

Unnatural is what goes against nature, contrary, not normal, lacking natural feelings, extremely cruel or wicked, artificial, affected, outlandish, weird, peculiar, strange, and natural is just the opposite. Natural is those things that are acceptable to God in man's life. Man has set back and allowed the thief and robber, Satan to come in and steal their hearts away from God.

A thief is a robber, one who secretly steals, takes another's property without permission or right, take or get by sly means, to move or put secretly or quietly, making no noise or disturbing sound, no excitement, tumult, but motionless or gently and mild a thief trains himself to be very quiet, free from noise you do not see him coming and you do not know where he goes. His mission is well planned. He comes in the night that no one sees him or recognize whom he is.

So as the Devil when he comes, he comes to steal, kill, and destroy. If man never sees him as he is or recognize him as he is, they will always be bound to the Devil.

He comes at the very weakest moments in man's lives, when they are too relaxed, free from trouble, trials, or tribulations, when they are tired and least expect him or right after a battle when their mind is on other things.

Satan is very subtle, faint and mysterious, mentally acute, cunning or crafty, elusively thin or fine, and delicate in meaning. He also is conniving, giving aid to doing wrong by pretending not to know or notice, to cooperate secretly.

Look at what he did Eve, he waited until she was alone and suggested things, not really being truthful, but he touched her emotions.

Many of God's children have been deceived by emotions, biological and psychological agitation in feeling; an instance of this is love, hate, sorrow, or fear. He plays with our senses, touching, feeling, tasting, smelling or seeing. Man is hereby warned of Satan's cunningness. He is a cutthroat.

His plan is to ruin our relationship with God, he is ruthless, he's cruel and a murderer from the beginning. He is not man's competition, but God's. He uses man to get to God because he cannot come to God except man brings him before God or allow him to go to God against man as a test.

Man need to wake up and know that sin does not love them and the sinner do not really love to sin, but because they are caught up in an emotional fleshly roller coaster,

Satan takes advantage of them. All of their habits are because they have acquired a taste for something. Man is born in a world of sin and they do not have to be taught how to sin. It is just a natural thing for them to lie, steal, cheat, and kill.

When a baby is born, they do not know what to do that is right, but they learn wrong easily without thinking about it.

Although they come in the world innocent, *in Genesis 6:2-4* God repented that he had made man, not that he created a man, man take on flesh and all that flesh has to offer him.

If what flesh has to offer is more than what they feed their spirit man, then flesh is what they will respond to.

Man brings men into the world, but they feed them death because they do not take time to put what God has given them into their off springs but, they allow them to eat of the junk of the world with no explanations.

Man can only impart what they know and understand. To see the world for what it is they must first see the giants in their lives that impair their sight so that they realize their own potential.

THE BUILT UP SOUL

Personal perception cause man to think more highly of themselves than they ought to.

It will cause them to feel like they can conquer the world but in the midst of their crises in life, they will buckle down because of their reliance on their emotions.

The Spirit of God must take precedence in their lives that he is the overtone of everything they do, for it is God the Father, God the Son, and God the Holy Ghost that is able to compete with the enemy that man has in this world.

THE BUILT UP SOUL

Who Is In Control God or Man

In the world man lives in, the question must be asked among them Who Is In Control? Man need to just let it go and relinquish control to the one that planted the seed in them. Is God in control or is man in control?

Control means man has given the power or authority to guide or manage, to check, test or verify by evidence or experiment, exercise restraining or directing influence over, a personality or spirit believed to actuate the utterance or performance of a spiritualist medium.

Control also means giving possession of what God put in man in the beginning that he becomes a living soul, which is God's Spirit. When mans flesh will die, God's Spirit goes back to him, it lives and never dies.

When man will let God be in control, leading and guiding him he allows God the ability to act or produce an effect in his life, have authority over his life, and man gives up the capacity and right to rule his own life.

When God is in control, man has given up his reign and his will and God's Spirit rules his spirit. In other words God control your life when you surrender your mind, body, and soul to him.

God is a Spirit and we must fall on our faces and admit that he is the God of the spirits of all flesh. *John 4:24* said that God is a spirit and they that worship him must worship him in spirit and in truth. Even Job in all of his afflictions continually

36

allowed God to be in control, he committed his cause to God, which do great and unsearchable, and marvelous things without number.

He asked a question in *Job11: 7*, canst thou by searching find out God? Canst thou find out the almighty unto perfection? God is great was Job's confession and we know him not, neither can the number of his years be searched out, we cannot comprehend, find him out and we cannot touch the almighty.

David in *Psalms 139:6*, declares that such knowledge is too wonderful for me, it is too high, I cannot attain unto it. When David rendered God control he declared in *Psalms145:3* that great is the Lord and greatly to be praised, and his greatness is unsearchable.

When man will realize who is in control, they will just let go. No man can know the Son of God, but the father, neither know any man the father save the son, and he to whomsoever the son will reveal him. In the depth of God is all wisdom and knowledge and it is unsearchable to man the riches thereof.

His judgments and his ways also are past finding out. Man is not God's mind or his counselor. The reason man can do anything in the earth realm is because of God's grace. The earth is full of God's riches but he is in control of it all for by his wisdom was all made that was made.

All wisdom and knowledge is his and he gives it to whomever he please, to those that will avail and give him control. He gives wisdom to the wise, and knowledge to them that knows understanding. So that man would give him control, he gave man control. Instead of man using what God gave him to bless him with, blessing, glory, wisdom, thanksgiving, honor, power, and might man has continually refused to give back that which he has received, and since God is not in control of his life and he will not let go of the things of the world,

God withholds his blessings. You can only be blessed when you bless. What is the heart of man is what man will speak. God is a Spirit and he wants total control of man so that he may pour out his Spirit in him as recorded in *Joel 2:28*.

Not only do he want to pour out into man his spirit, but have free course in his life. God allows the course of nature to run in one's life rather they choose the good or bad of it.

When man does not render control to God, he is quenching his Spirit and this grieves God. Soon man will have to give up meekly and quietly and see God for who he really is, their creator instead of being haughty, contrite and disobedient to his Word.

Man can only surrender to God his mind, soul, body and spirit that God wants to control. He gave man dominion over everything else in the earth. He was not in control of God's creation because God created man to the praise of his glory.

Man needs to feed his spirit everyday through the reading and studying of his creator.

THE BUILT UP SOUL

In the beginning was the Word, and then the Word became flesh. God is his Word and his Word is his mind. How can he control us without the surrendering of a man's natural mind, body and soul?

Can man tell you of a surety why rain falls and from where it falls? He can because of God's wisdom predict that rain will fall but even then the clouds can change.

Can man tell you why it rains on one side of the street and the sun shines on the other side? Who is it that is in control that can make man with no man's help?

Proverbs 3:5 says in all thy ways acknowledge him and he shall direct thy paths. In all things, rejoice in the Lord and let our moderation be known to him.

Be careful for nothing but in everything by prayer and supplication with thanksgiving let your request be made known unto God.

How can we feel comfortable going to him to ask anything of him when we have not been in relationship with him? If man does not love God, how can he love his fellow man?

They cannot properly associate what is proper and what is not, because there is no reverence in their speech, reverence in their walk, or in their talk. God's man is angelic and he protects because he provides a spiritual covering for the rest of mankind.

His strength and faith is in the Word of God. He then needs to look farther than the cover to seen what is inside. What is inside is his Creator, not the creature. Man is worthy of his hire, but will he render himself to his Master?

God will give him a reason to live and he will know that God's Word is health to his bones. Inside of his bones is marrow that will keep his offspring that his seed has produced.

The flesh is nothing without the Spirit of God. It is a mess, it's like a biscuit with whipped cream.

THE BUILT UP SOUL

The Breath Of Life; God Gave It

It was God that begin the life of man and only God should have control of the life of man. We must understand that even if we face abuse in life. Its not God's doing; so don't be angry with God. Listen we were special made

Genesis 2:5b-7 for the Lord God had not caused it to rain upon the earth, and there was not a man to till the ground, but there went up a mist from the earth and watered the whole face of the ground and the Lord God formed man of the dust of the ground and breathed into his nostrils the breath of life; and man became a living soul.

The breath of life; it was the Holy Ghost, the breath of God that gave life to man as we know it. Man usually attribute their lives to the parents. God chooses who we are birth forth to in this world. God is the giver of all life; the good and bad.

God made all things good but that which was made; followed that evil one Satan to be known as bad. That's how evil was attributed to God's making good and evil.

Children, we don't know how our life will be lived out or how we will depart this life and be returned to God. If we are alive, that mean our earthly parents didn't abort us, so be thankful to God for them even if we feel life wasn't as we thought it should be.

Ephesians 1:1-13, we are here for the will of God; be faithful to the call. We are blessed with all spiritual blessings in heavenly places in Christ. We were chosen in Him before the foundation of the world that we should be Holy and without blame before him in love.

He predestined us unto the adoption of children by Jesus Christ according to the good pleasure of his Will. He made us accepted in the beloved by means of his grace. We have redemption through his blood, the forgiveness of sins by the richness of that grace.

He gives us his wisdom and prudence that can only be found in his Word and breathe upon by his Spirit. He make known to us the mystery of his Will by means of the Holy Ghost according to his good pleasure which he has purposed in Himself

Its in his timing that the dispensation of time will be fulfilled in us. God will bring into fruition in our lives what he purposed for all men that we be to the praise of his glory that we receive the inherited promise of eternal life. On our way we must learn to trust in Christ! Its going to take some work on our part! Why?

God the Father worked and did his part in the life of man. Jesus The Christ did his part and the Holy Ghost did his part! So now what are we going to do? How are we going to act?

God Said "*Let There Be*", the Holy Spirit heard the Word, moved at the Word, pleased and perfected what God said. What is our purpose in earth? We were created to the praise of God's glory to bring glory to God. Let no one steal our joy in life. Know who we are and whose we are.

Life, we are a seed planted and breathed upon by the Holy Ghost. God created man a spiritual being but he in that state served not God purpose for him in the earth. Man could not reproduce that which was needed to upkeep and in replenishing the earth.

God's spiritual man was alive but he was no earthly good. People even today enjoy being good for nothing. It was the Word in the beginning spoken and breathed upon by God that gave us life as we know it. The Spirit gave life to everything in the earth at the speaking of the

THE BUILT UP SOUL

Word. God had first reproduced himself spiritually. Man was to reproduce God in their offspring.

Man then would give life in the Spirit and flesh to offspring; but then they forget to reproduce spiritual things in the children. The Holy Ghost was breathed on the inside. Man celebrate taking care of the outer man but forget the inner man which can only be kept alive by the Holy Ghost. They don't know Him.

The Holy Ghost is a He; God is a He! Just like the Holy Ghost is an unexplainable act of God; it is a very unspoken act in the world today because it is very much not understood by man. The things of God are spiritually discerned!

We have life because God wants the glory out of our lives! Give Him the glory today no matter what we face in this life. One day we will have that perfect day and trouble will have to flee!

Walk the walk, talk the talk, keep our heads lifted up and we will surely see that blessed day when we walk out of darkness into the light.

THE BUILT UP SOUL

Innocence, Betrayal, and Mistrust

We must look at life as weighing things in the balance. Life has balance and in the balance of life we will find abuse trapped therein. Man however must not allow abuse to overtake them. We must look to God who is the Author and finisher of our faith.

Many children as I have been, has been abused in some form. So many have been robbed of their innocence, been betrayed by those they love and put confidence in. Then as they travel through life as an adult they too will be abusive in most cases.

Many face abuse because they seek help from the wrong source. Parent although they mess up, don't want there children messed up. We are to thank God for our parents. They may mess their life up but don't yours to be like theirs. Many think to give up their children when they find themselves in a mess is good; but not necessarily so.

Thank God for them and their mess ups! Grow from them, don't become a repeat act. A father gives seed and a mother receives the seed but they allowed the seed to grow and not abort it. Then there is now me and you; nine months later. They are to feed us both naturally and spiritually.

In America today we van look and see a backslidden America. Jesus is on the outskirts of everything. Parents forgot how to pray. There is hardly any prayers at home, school, or church in a lot of cases.

Though we walk in the flesh, we do not war after the flesh (I Cor. 10:3-6). The weapons of our warfare are not carnal, but mighty through God, to the pulling down of strongholds. Casting down wicked imaginations and every high thing that exalts itself against the knowledge of God.

THE BUILT UP SOUL

We are in the face of abuse but we must war against those things that come to take away our soul. How many times do we find ourselves wanting to do right but evil is ever present to stop us? Oh and how we abuse the word; but! Meaning; however on the other hand, nevertheless, on the contrary, except, other than, otherwise then, I would do right, but you know. Yes, God knows too!

We use too many excuses for not doing what is right and proper. When they fail to accomplish in life what is expected or desired they rely on excuses. They rely on excuses for not living right.

People regard not moral practical things, nor what's right and wrong in behavior, nor conforming to the standard or established order and blame abuse for being a misfit in life.

Man is abused, innocent, betrayed and have much mistrust of others but what is right and wrong in moral, practical applications must be applied in every area of life.

God has a sustained legal established order man is to follow.

THE BUILT UP SOUL

From Darkness To Light

In life we will learn some things! From the time a child is born in this world; they are learning. We learn how that we should live life in this world. What we learn early in life has everything to do with how we will leave the earth. A child learns what the live and live what they learn.

When Adam was created in this world, he knew nothing of the world. He just roamed around in the world with Eve at his side free from the contaminants of the earth. God had made them in the earth but they knew not the world they were in. But thanks to the mean subtle demonic force; Satan they would soon like a new born baby learn some things about where they were.

They were sinless, full of light. There were no darkness in them for they were the light of the world. They were full of God. They set in a high place, a city that could not be hid for their purity illuminated the earth.

The light of the body is the eye; therefore when thine eye is single Jesus said in *Luke 11:34* thy whole body also is full of light; but when thine eye is evil, thy body also is full of darkness.

When we God's created and made beings realize who we really are; we too will choose light over darkness. It was in God we had life; its still like that today. When life as we know it is passed; we still have life in the Spirit that man was; in his first state. Adam and Eve were created first spiritually, then made naturally.

God's light shined through them even after they were put inside made bodies; different in nature with different functions. Samuel said in *I Samuel 20:3* truly as the Lord liveth and as thy soul liveth, there is but one step between me and death.

Because of the spiritual death Adam and Eve brought forth to man, death now both naturally and spiritually happens. Death is imminent and we know not when it will come. We are in the world but not of the world. How death finds us and our life lived determines our resting place away from earth.

The light of God that shined forth within them was replaced with emptiness and darkness; yet they comprehended it not.

They knew a change came because they found themselves naked as they always was. But something happened and they knew it; but didn't know until God spoke his disapproval of their actions.

God still tell man today of our sins. Repent them and quit doing them! We are better than what the world have to offer us!

Be the light with the light God sent to bring man out of darkness once again! Hear one day God say welcome home thy good and faithful servant; enter into rest.

THE BUILT UP SOUL

The Fix It Man

Jesus the fix it man came to earth, not really a stranger in the earth for He had always been here. In the beginning was the Word, and the Word was with God, and the Word was God *(St. John 1:1)*. God is the Creator but He used all of Himself, Father, Word, and Spirit working to get things done

God in the beginning spoke the Word creating the Heavens and the Earth (*Genesis 1:1*). God spoke the Word and the Holy Spirit moved at the hearing of the Word and got things done.

Jesus; Best of the best of all the Godly, the whole five fold ministry. He fulfilled them all. *Ephesians 4:11* God had given some Apostles, and some Prophets, and some Evangelists, and some Pastors and Teachers. All would need Him to carry them to finishing the work. We are not to fear for Jesus didn't leave us comfortless.

He leads us through the leading and guiding of his Holy Spirit that is the continuator of the Work of Christ in the earth. *John 14:16* Jesus said He would pray the Father and He shall give you another Comforter that may abide with you forever. He it is that would teach us all things in Jesus Name!

Jesus was sent to man and fulfilled all of these offices that man would be perfected in them as He was to work toward perfecting Saints for the work of the ministry and the edifying of the body of Christ. HE would carry within Him all of the nine spiritual gifts (*1 Corinthians 12:8-10*) and the nine fruit of the Spirit (*Galatian 5:22*).

THE BUILT UP SOUL

Why would He need to come? Genesis 1:27 so *God created man in his own image*, in the *image of God created he him; male and female* created he them. *God wanted himself back; so he sent Himself back to fix man back to Himself!*

Genesis 2:7 and the Lord God *formed man* of the dust of the ground, and *breathed into his nostrils the breath of life*: and *man became a living soul*. God through Jesus caused man to breathe new life again.

Isaiah 43:7 even every one that is *called by my name*; for *I have created him for my glory*, I have formed him; yea, I have made him.

Ephesians 1:4-6 according as he hath chosen us to him before the foundation of the world, that *we should be holy* and *without blame before him* in love; having *predestinated* us unto the *adoption of children* by Jesus Christ to himself, *according to the good pleasure of his will, to the praise of the glory of his grace*, wherein he hath made us accepted in the beloved.

What Is My Purpose? God has made it plain what man's purpose in the earth is; to *glorify Him* as their Creator, be *fruitful and multiply in the earth bringing forth seed that may reproduce after its own kind, man and woman producing* children, *providing* and *protecting* them from all hurt and harm.

We were *walking, talking, living epistles.* Man was to *keep the earth*; God's Creation. On the *spiritual side* we are to *produce saints* through the *process of a new birth* to *save souls*. Once we have been saved and recommitted our lives to Christ *we must become soul winners reaching*

49

out to save the lost at any cost; even at the *cost* of our *own life.*

We are here to work the work of Christ, walk the walk of *faith* and *be the sons of God*. Our *purpose* is to do the *will of the Father* after the *likeness of Christ Jesus*.

Genesis 1:28 and God blessed them and God said unto them, *be fruitful and multiply and replenish* the earth and subdue it; and *have dominion over* the fish of the sea, and over the fowl of the air, and over every living thing that moveth upon the earth.

Ephesians 1:9-12 having *made known* unto us *the mystery of his will*, according to his *good pleasure* which he hath *purposed in himself*; that in the dispensation of the fullness of times He might gather together in one *all things in Christ,* both which are in heaven and which are on earth; even in him: in whom also we have obtained an inheritance, being predestinated according to the purpose of him who worketh all things after the counsel of his own will; that we should be to the praise of his glory, who first trusted in Christ.

Man was *filled with excuse* after Adam disobeyed. *Gen. 3:12* and the man said, the woman whom thou gave to be with me, she gave me of the tree and I did eat. The *blame game* started and went on from there. Man had the can't help its since then. God gave Jesus a charge to cancel the blame game.

The Contract, Redeem Them. Jesus Christ Shed Blood to redeem man in answering the charge of God.

The Blood sacrifice Jesus made was for the whole of mankind. Naturally blood is the fluid which circulates in the principal vascular system of animate creatures conveying nourishment in all parts of the body and brings with it all waste materials (products).

Jesus brought back life to the Spirit to have a direct flow in keeping us alive spiritually in proper relationship with God as we live in earth.

What Did Happen? Leviticus 17:11, 14 we are told that *life is in the blood.* Life as we know it is *the breath of God.*

When man, one man Adam *disobeyed God by eating* fruit from the *named tree of life*, he *accepted sin* for the *whole of man*. So now man is not only *born into sin*, but *conceived in sin* to.

The *God given charge to Jesus brought back*, *redeemed us into right relationship with our Heavenly Father again.*

In *Deut. 12:23* we read that the blood is in the life. The new blood man can and has acquired through Christ is the choice to choose right over wrong. A life of obedience that came through Jesus *blood sacrifice took away all excuses* to sin. He went on to *shed his blood* making his life a *ransom* for all.

Now Paul said in *Romans 1:20* for the *invisible things* of *him* from the *creation of the world* are *clearly seen, being understood by the things that are made*, even his *eternal power and Godhead;* so that they are *without excuse*.

As we *come to know Christ* we come into the *unity* of the *faith and the knowledge* of the *Son of God* unto a *perfect man*. Unto the measure of the stature of the fullness of Christ. He is the *strength* of man. *He is risen* so we too can rise above sin. When we know the truth we are not so *easily deceived by the tactics* and *plans of the Devil*; they enemy of our soul.

Jesus shared life with man again with the God given charge to go and *bring restoration* of *the Spirit of God* to man again. It *took shed blood* as a final sacrifice to *make the atonement needed* for this to happen.

The blood applied tell the death angel to pass over. They see Him and honor his presence in our life. He had a charge from his Father to save man from death, destruction and Hell's fire. *Death is the last enemy in the life of man*

We are **back into proper relationship with God** because **Jesus came and made atonement** for us and we are **new creatures** in Him, *II Cor. 5:17-19*. **He is our hope and was our last sacrifice**. He is our "**fix it man**"! He will if given the opportunity will fix all that ails man.

When we are **weary**, **weak**, and **feel worthless**, physically or mentally fatigued, impatient or tired, or angry He will *help us regroup our self*. *He was charged by God* to bring forth deliverance to man. He was charged to heal man's woes. He was to *set us free from Satan's bondages*.

We are free *because of His living Sacrifice* made for us at the Cross. Jesus *took* his *God given charge* and *ran with it* just for us. *He is the best!*

Jesus, *the second Adam* meaning *one born of God,* as Genesis teaches that man is in a peculiar sense *the image of his "Divine Creator"* and meant to rule under God over the rest of the created world; that the gift of a blessed immortality was within his reach.

Man's moral development could come only through trial. Jesus flesh was put to the test. He overcame all the desires to fulfill the flesh Satan presented Him. So now man don't have to sin, they choose too!

THE BUILT UP SOUL

Man Created In Holiness

Who Am I is a question asked by men and women everywhere. Even children ask this question and look for answers that can only come from knowing who God is in our lives. Who we look at and see in the mirror is not who we are as far as Christ is concerned.

Who God made us to be is that spirit created and placed on the inside of man. *God breathe on man* and *man became a living soul*. We are *living souls that walk around in bodies of flesh* that was *made of dust and water* from the earth.

Why Am I Here is a question many wonder about. We don't know why we are here or why God sent us into this world of corruption. God created man to the praise of His Glory. We were created to praise God and give Him Glory throughout the earth.

Where Am I Going; the question is do we know where we are going after this life? Do we know what we are doing in this life to take us to the next life? God in his Word has given us specifics about this life and the life to come.

No matter which life we decide; we are going to partake of it either heaven or hell. There is life after we depart this earth. *Who we trust in* while we live determines life tomorrow.

We have *heard* in one way or the other the Word of Truth which is the gospel of our salvation. If we *believe the Word* after *hearing* it then we are *saved with a promise* of *eternal life* if we endure to the end (*Matthew 24:13*).

If we *reject the Word* when we hear it we have a *promise* of *hell and damnation for eternity*.

THE BUILT UP SOUL

There is a war going on inside of us that keeps us from God or brings us closer to Him.
Galatians 5:16-17 this I say then, *walk in the Spirit,* and ye *shall not fulfill the lust of the flesh*. For the *flesh lusteth against the Spirit,* and the *Spirit against the flesh*: and these are *contrary the one to the other*; so that ye cannot do the things that ye would.

Galatians 6:8 for *he that soweth to his flesh* shall of the *flesh reap corruption*; but he that soweth to the Spirit shall of the *Spirit reap life everlasting*.

When Will I Know I Am Saved? The Lord our God is holy, are we holy? He is the King eternal in heaven and in earth, do we believe Him to be? He is immortal and invisible, the only wise God that we live to bring honor and glory to forever and ever; do we? Do we believe that there is none besides Him?

Jesus said we must be born again of the Spirit because the law of God is perfect and we can only be perfect in Him. We must be found written in the Lamb's book of life. When I confess with my mouth the Lord Jesus and believe in my heart, turn away from sin then I am saved. The law of the Lord is perfect, converting the soul; the testimony of the Lord is sure.

Isaiah 59:2 but your *iniquities have separated* between you and your God, and your sins have *hid his face* from you, that he will not hear

Romans 3:23 for all have sinned, and come short of the glory of God.

God created us that we praise Him in the beauty of holiness. He created us to bring glory to Him. He then made us to take special care of His Creation! that's all inclusive of His created being He breathed

Himself into. He wants to be our inside guide once more. How do He want to accomplish that?

Salvation is an inside job. We are living Epistles, a letter to be read among men everywhere we go. Give Him you today and He will make Himself known to you!

Be ye holy for I am Holy said the Lord.

I Corinthians 3:16 know ye not that ye are the temple of God, and that the Spirit of God dwells in you.

If we love God that first loved us we want to be what He is; Holy. We need the grace of the Lord Jesus Christ, and the love of God and the communion of the Holy Ghost to be with us that we can be holy. After all that God has done for us we should want to please Him in every way we can. We live a life of Christ not by might or power but by the Spirit of God.

We live Holy by following God's Word that has been tried and found to be true. We live on the rock of Christ's work in the earth which was perfect; for all his ways are judgment, a God of truth and without iniquity, just and right so why wouldn't we want to be like Him.

Romans 14:12 so then every one of us shall give account of himself to God.

We should be holy because we are angels on assignment in the earth. What has God told us to do that we have not done? What have He told us to do that we allocated to someone else? Instead of doing it like God says we appoint someone and commission them to do what God has charged us to do and it fails. How many times have we stood in

THE BUILT UP SOUL

God's way? But when we keep ourselves pure and clean before the Lord we are ready and available to be used by Him. Some things we go through we would never have gone through it had we remained faithful in our call to be holy.

Sin keeps us away from God and the things of God. Sin says we did wrong, guilt says I am wrong, and it keeps us hiding from God and man.

Adam and Eve hid when God came looking for them because they sinned. Why would they hide; God had been all they knew! They realized another being had come forth that they knew not! Flesh was alive!

In God's likeness and image they were pure, clean and ready for communion with God each day but their curiosity drove them far away into another realm away from God. For the first time their eyes radiated a naked body before them. They had been stripped of their innocence.

Throughout the Word of God we have men that loved God too but succumb to the flesh time and time again. We have graciously helped Satan to build up a wall within us that blocks the Kingdom of God to rule in our heart. Sin is on an all time high but God has a way of calling man back. He gives second chances.

What a task! The kingdom of hell has enlarged itself. Satan is on his job to deceive as many people he can to make his kingdom greater than God's. We have the awesome assignment to not allow this to happen on our watch.

If we observe we will see that sin is more rampant and open today than twenty years ago. People disrespect God with no fear today. We need to take another look at the assignment and be careful not to get caught up in the web of sin. We need to be more watchful, alert, mindful, attentive, observant and wary of the sin that happens in our lives in and around us. We have a call to go and compel men to come to Christ. What are we doing?

Genesis 19:1-2 and there came two Angels to Sodom at evening time; and Lot sat in the gate of Sodom and Lot seeing them rose up to meet them; and he bowed himself with his face toward the ground. And he said, behold now, my lords turn in, I pray you, into your servant's house, and tarry all night, and wash your feet, and ye shall rise up early, and go on your ways, and they said, Nay; but we will abide in the street all night.

We should be holy and remain holy because we are earthly angels with a heavenly mission just like the angels God sent to Lot's house. They were as men in the earth. Because of their Holy nature in heaven they were able to be dispatched to earth to save Lot and his family.

God wants to still save families from the horrific mess sin causes. He wants me and you to be his angels on assignment in the earth to get the work done. He uses our mouth to speak his Word. He need access to our feet, eyes, hands and ears to move Him about in the earth.

Genesis 19:10-13 but the men put forth their hand and pulled Lot into the house to them and shut the door. And they smote the men that were at the door of the house with blindness, both small and great; so that they wearied themselves to find the door. And the men said unto Lot; hast thou here any besides? Son in law, and thy sons, and thy daughters, and whatsoever thou hast in the city, bring them out of this place. For we will destroy this place because the cry of them is waxen (increased, grown, enlarged, expanded, and flourished), great before the face of the Lord; and the Lord hath sent us to destroy it.

The men that came knocking at Lot's door were seeking out the two men (Angels) that came into Lot's house that night. Lot offered them his daughters but that was the way God ordained man to be. God created and made a wife for Adam with his rib and laid her at Adam's side.

God never ordained marriage any other way. If it is found to be another way it is an abominable act and anyone that succumbs to this abomination will surely die. To them that knows to do good (right) and does not it is sin. We are not to have our good evil spoken of.

These acts the men of Sodom was caught up in was not just sin but an abomination. The odor smelling in that city was contemptible, disgusting, horrible, loathsome, repugnant and offensive in God's nostrils. Their doings came before God as despicable.

What drove these acts was wickedness. They had given themselves over to this evil spirit and thought they were okay; well their city was destroyed with them in it because of this immorality. Does this sound familiar in our day in this country? What about in the world in which we live?

These acts man indulge in or involve themselves in tell God that they don't like what He has made them to be; it is blasphemy against the Holy Ghost that gave life to the body. It is a total denial and calls God, His Word and Spirit a liar, and deceiver. It's an outcry, complaint or objection. This lifestyle lived is wrong as two left shoes on our feet. Fornication and adultery is wrong too! The one is unnatural and the other is a natural sin but one is outside of God's Order. Neither is too be upheld!

They told Lot to take his wife and thy two daughters, which are here that they be not consumed in the iniquity of the city. Instead of going on and doing as they were told they lingered; so that the Angels had to take them by the hand and bring them to the outskirts of the city that their lives were spared.

Yes God will forcibly save us at his promise to get his work done. Why though does God have to force his mercy and favor on us? For best results follow instructions. God have a hard time blessing some of us because we are disobedient to what He has told us to do and we think too much.

We know everything where no one can tell us anything that will benefit us. We rely on what a man says rather than God. God favor is more than money. It is a blessing that we would want to have.

God's divine favor is declared upon us because of our faithfulness in obedience to God's assignments. God had made a promise to His people that in blessings He would bless us and in multiplying I will multiply thy seed as the stars in heaven. He also promised us that the gate of our enemies we shall possess.

Sin is an enemy and when we look around seems as though it's having a field day in the life of the Saints of Jesus Christ. The Lord is our strength. He is our song and is become our salvation. We can't make it in our own strength; we need Jesus.

THE BUILT UP SOUL

God makes us to lie down in green pastures; so what make us think that He will come against us with His great power when we are so weak? God put his strength in us that we walk in the paths of righteousness. It is He that restores our soul unto Himself. He leads us beside the still waters. God does all these things that we being glory to His Name.

Our problem is this; God gives us assignments and we want to build a Church. It's no wonder Churches are failing everywhere and men are backsliding every day. God will bring forth his righteousness, give us courage in the day, strengthen our hearts and bless us to continue to hope in Him.

God upholds us if we keep the righteous path. We can wash the curse off of us through obedience to the Word. When we submit ourselves to the Word of God and walk in his Divine Will He will bless us with blessings we will never forget.

Don't allow the book of the law depart out of our mouths. Lot was blessed and delivered because of God's promise to Abraham; Abraham staggered not at the Word. We won't stagger either when we keep the law of God, His Commandments, observe to do accordingly the whole Word, and meditate on the Word day and night.

If we do these things just like Lot and his family we will spend our days in prosperity, our years in pleasure. This is the favor of God; Divine blessings.

Lot and his family were right in the midst of the stench of sin that polluted the city of Sodom but they still remained faithful to keep the Commandments of God in their heart. Length of days, long life, and peace was added unto them. If we want the blessings of the Lord that make us rich with no sorrow added to it we must obey and follow the Word; living and written.

We are Angels on assignment just as these two were. We have a charge to keep and a race to win. The race is not given to the swift or to the strong but to them that endure to the end; the same shall be saved. Obedience in the natural element that brings us into submission to the Father and He in turn blesses us with spiritual blessings.

God will bring forth our righteousness as the light. He will uphold us in the time of need when we are of a good courage and realize that God through our hope in Him will strengthen our hearts to take us far and near. We have God's holiness.

As God's Angels on assignment we must follow the plan of God for our lives to the utmost. Make sure we gain a complete knowledge of our assignment and not linger around with it but work it. In our assignment we too as the Angels may face opposition but we have to exercise restraint and allow God to have front and center stage in our lives.

It is God that is able to make us stand. We operate in His gifts but it is He that works them. The weapons of our warfare are not carnal, but mighty through God to the pulling down of strongholds. When we go on assignment we must know that it is God's battle and He will fight it to bring it to an expected end.

It is God that works in us both to will and to do of His good pleasure. We are not our own but we belong solely to God; even the gifts we operate in belongs to Him, He gives good and perfect gifts.

THE BUILT UP SOUL

We are kept by the power of God through faith unto salvation ready to be revealed in this time we live in. Everything done in the dark will be revealed and judged.

God's Divine power has given us all things that pertain to life and godliness, through the knowledge of Him that has called us to glory and virtue. We have been given promises; exceeding great and precious promises at that. This has been done so that we might be partakers of the divine nature, having escaped the corruption that is in the world through lust. If we be faithful unto death we will receive a crown of life.

God will in the meantime heal all of our diseases, forgive our iniquities, redeem our life from destruction, crown us with loving kindness and tender mercies, satisfy our mouth with good things and renew our youth like the eagles.

When we are on assignment there is no good thing God will withhold from us that believe. Eye has not seen, nor ear heard, neither have it entered in the hearts of man the things which God has prepared for them that love Him.

When we keep His Commandments, walk in His Ways, do His Will and continue to obey all of these we will enter into the Holy of Holies and get the spiritual help we need to continue the assignment God called us to.

THE BUILT UP SOUL

God Charged Officers

It's time we find out who we are. We as Christians have work to do. We are called, chosen, appointed and anointed to offer salvation to man and build up their souls with the Word of God. The office of the Christian is not what we think it is but what God says it is.

An office what is it? It is a call, a special duty, charge or position conferred by an exercise of authority, and for a purpose of responsibility to an executive authority.

There is a prescribed form or service of worship associated with that call for a divine office. It calls for religious or social ceremonial observance and reminds one of what they ought to or must do.

Whether a call to office is spiritual or natural there is some assigned and assumed duties associated with it and its main function is something done for another and some particular kind of service is supplied.

The officer in the office will be giving some kind of directives to maintain and improve upon some person place or thing throughout the duration of service. Who are we? We are the officers of God; agents charged with an office that involves trust, faith, honesty, obedience, suffering, persecution, and sometimes death.

Are we ready to find out who we are and what we have been called to and for what reason?

We as Christians, the believers of Christ has been called to prepare the way for Christ's return. We are officials in the army of God, and the Holy Ghost is our appointed Captain that leads and guides us into all areas of truth and around the enemy of our souls. We too however have a part to play in the work of Salvation. After we have accepted Christ as Savior we need the Holy Ghost. No one can give it to you or make you get it. We need the Holy Ghost, the Spirit of God upon us to do a work that we ourselves in the flesh cannot do because it is not a work of the flesh.

What do we mean by we need? Need means it is a requirement, it is necessary, essential, imperative, mandatory and important. We can do nothing except God breathe His Spirit on what we are doing. In Him we live, we move, and we have our being. Without Him nothing made; was made.

God is the Creator of the earth and the fullness thereof belongs to Him. It is He that has made us and not we ourselves so we don't belong to ourselves, our parents, man, woman, elected officials, preacher, teacher, or any other.

We need the Spirit of God; not man. When God created man, man was created in God's image a spirit being, male and female just like what God was. After finishing His work in Creation God said all of His work was good. He rested the seventh day.

On the eighth day having given his created beings instructions as to live in the earth He realized that in the state man was in He could not use him in the office he had called him to. This created being could not keep the earth or reproduce in it in their created state.

God as He wondered how this newly created being would be an able worker in the upkeep of the earth, something happened. The earth gave up some dust and water. The earth He had created worked with Him in the process of making man an earthen vessel for the created spiritual being. He would make a man of the dust and water. When God finished He put the created male and female spirit being inside of the flesh but yet the man He made flesh was not a lively being.

So God breathe on the body His Spirit and man became a living soul. He was no longer just a dead man lying on the ground. Why do we need the Spirit of God? The Spirit of God makes us a live spirit made flesh being. We were first spiritual then flesh was added. But even then that one body had two components inside of it that could not work.

There were now two entities in one body; male and female. Adam's helpmeet was yet on the inside of him. He gave birth to the female when God took a rib out of his side. the female out of him. The male now called man was a living being and had the female still on the inside of him. God saw that Adam was lonely and was the only being that did not have an outward mate so He took a rib out of Adam's side and formed the woman up to the outside of his body.

Woman no longer dwell inside of man but to his side; *Genesis 1:26 Genesis 2:10*. They now had two distinct offices with two different positions but yet they both were still one flesh and had one Master and Maker; God. God gave Adam a woman to wife; a female.

Although they were now two entities in two bodies they still did not know they were different. They were yet spiritual beings in earthen bodies not knowing each other in a fleshly state. How do we know this?

THE BUILT UP SOUL

When Satan presented himself they were in the Garden and Adam with his wife stood around and I can imagine Eve was looking upon the tree in the midst of the Garden and playing with a snake. At this time we can assume that the snake was not a snake as we know them today; vicious.

The snake (*serpent*) walked upright like a human before he was cursed to forever crawl on his belly for allowing Satan to use him. Why was Eve talking to a snake anyway when Adam her companion was right there that she could have talked to. My imagination takes me to the point where they were discussing how beautiful the fruit looked and how harmless it seemed.

This is the point where Satan saw his entrance into the conversation. He had her full attention now and he sought to beguile her where he could deceive Adam. He knew what God had told them and saw his way in to trick them.

Up until this point he waited on the opportunity for her to take her attention off of her husband and God. Her eyes wandered from the beacon path to the beauty of what the tree had upon it. She also gave her attention and ears to an animal rather than her husband. This caused her to hear what she needed not hear; a lie.

She left her call by giving attention to the wrong things; giving her sight to things forbidden and her ears to hear what sounded like it might be true. Not only that she moved her hands in the direction of the enemy, touched the untouchable, and ate. How did Adam get deceived then?

He saw that Eve had eaten and nothing happened to change their condition as God had said. God told them that in the day they ate of the forbidden fruit of the tree in the midst of the Garden they would know good and evil; *Genesis 2:9, 3:3, 3:11.*

Satan told them that God knew that they would be like Him if they ate of the forbidden fruit, **Genesis 3:5**. He always adds some lie to truth to make things seem like they are real and true. He still uses the same trick on man today.

He still uses the woman to deceive man and usurp his authority in the earth. Adam didn't stand his ground in putting Eve in check for her disobedience for God had given them commandment while they were still spiritual beings outside of flesh.

How soon had he forgotten what God said and listened to the woman as she readily put the fruit in his mouth and he did eat. She disobeyed Adam and Adam disobeyed God. They both was hiding when God came looking for them, **Genesis 3:9-10**. Sin will make us hide out; it stops us from being who God called us to be.

Sin tears down the office God calls us to. That's why we need the Spirit of God and not man. Man can be deceived and woman too! Adam and Eve didn't have the anointing that went along with the work because they weren't aware of Satan's devices but we are and there is no excuse.

Jesus took away the excuse man had to sin in the flesh or Spirit. The first man and woman had to learn of things blindly but we in this time know of what's good and what s evil; we know right from wrong. We know of Satan, evil spirits and spiritual wickedness. We must choose the way we will take. Jesus brought back the office of choice to man.

THE BUILT UP SOUL

All of the Prophets spoke of Christ coming in one way or another, but Isaiah in *Isaiah 61:1-6* prepared us and described the office in which Christ would come. The Spirit of the Lord God is upon me; because the Lord hath anointed me to preach good tidings.

But ye shall be named then unto the meek; he hath sent me to bind up the brokenhearted to proclaim liberty to the captives, and the opening of the prison to them that are bound; to proclaim the acceptable year of the Lord, and the day of vengeance of our God, to comfort all that mourn; to appoint unto them that mourn in Zion, to give unto them beauty for ashes, the oil of joy for mourning, the garment of praise for the spirit of heaviness; that they might be called trees of righteousness, the planting of the Lord that he might be glorified: and they shall build the old wastes, they shall raise up the former desolations, and they shall repair the waste cities, the desolation of many generations. And strangers shall stand and feed your flocks, and the sons of the alien shall be your plowmen and your vinedressers.

But ye shall be named the Priests of the Lord; men shall call you the Ministers of our God; ye shall eat the riches of the Gentiles and in their glory shall ye boast yourselves. We the people of God have that same call to our portions today.

We have that same God promise today that if we be found faithful that we would be like Job; we would have double for our shame and for confusion we will rejoice in our portions of possessing joy double.

We know that God directs our works in truth and is covenant to it; God is a Spirit and we worship Him

THE BUILT UP SOUL

in Spirit and in Truth; they go together. We need the anointing that goes with the work. We need God to apply the oil of gladness to us that joy rings out in times of trouble, strength to do the work given and some power of endurance.

We need the power for salvation shown by Christ. Just as God anointed Jesus of Nazareth to do a work He has anointed us today to work just as much as Christ did in the time he walked in the earth. He needs us anointed to prepare the way of the Lord.

It's no time to rest up on God when our necks are under persecution. The world as then is in an identity crisis. There are relationship struggles and issues that can take us to hell. Our desires are in the wrong places; we don't call on God like we use to. Have we forgotten who it is that have made us?

Man's passion for life is after the flesh and not Spirit. Christ is coming back for a spiritual house; one not made with hands. We must have balance in our lives, and if we do not it's almost time to stop pretending and going to hell first class. Have we forgotten that we need more of God and less of the flesh?

Many have it backwards; but God is looking and the Angels are booking. The more of God we get the less of the flesh we desire and vice versa; the more of man we get the more of the flesh we desire. Man's nature is after the flesh therefore we are to seek for the nature of God.

When we find the more of God we find ourselves in a closer relationship with Him and we come under our Creator and appreciate the redemption he has given us through Christ. We come to realize we need help.

If God does not help us there is no restoration of man in this life. We however still have a responsibility to fulfill the call God has given us or have we forgotten?

It's time we take a self-inventory of our own salvation that we should be taking very serious. Are we perfect? No! But we can be perfect and perfect the things we know to do right. Giving in to the pressures of life will keep us bound and eventually destroy the whole of mankind.

Deliverance is a process and our steps are ordered by the Lord. Take one step at a time and refuse to stay in the muck and mire of life Lodebar brings our way. Understand the process and stay with God. Jesus Christ himself came down from Heaven just as Isaiah prophesied he would and had to stay the course; what about us? He had to confess any shortcomings as a man and know the deficiencies of a man; have we forgotten?

Jesus wept; although it was for us, it showed he had love for us. In all of our uncleanness, nastiness, and disobedience He still came to die for our sin.

Repentance is to the Christian as food is to the body, it is a must. It brings us to the heart of God and God's Spirit keeps the flesh under subjection to the perfection and providence of God. .

Repentance brings us face to face with God. Repentance keeps up righteous before God. Have we forgotten what it takes to get to God and stay there? Within the call to an office in Christ we must keep a repentant spirit to keep the Spirit of God alive in us.

God's mercy brought us. He has not given up on us. Our labor is not in vain. Laboring brings forth thanksgiving; every day is a day of thanksgiving. Have we forgotten what Paul said in **Philippians 4:13** that I can do all things through Christ that strengthens me and **Philippians 4:19** but my God shall supply all of my need according to His riches in Christ Jesus.

Have we forgotten that God said he would pour us out blessings that we would not have room enough to receive? Have we forgotten that Jesus is on his way again? Have we forgotten that because of God's love for us that He is vexed at the way we live our lives outside of his confines?

Watchmen it's time to speak up; we are to never hold our peace day or night concerning those things that please or displease God. It's no time to be silent we must be about establishing God's peace in the earth. It is time to rest but make God a praise in the earth.

The Lord is our right hand and He is the arm of our strength. Surely God will no more give our corn to be meat for our enemy and the sons of the stranger shall not drink our wine for the which we has labored for. Our labor will bring about the praises of the Lord from others.

We bring the Holiness of the Lord to man. It's a time of preparation; preparation for heaven on earth. We must go through not for ourselves but for God's use and we will be called Sought Out, a city not forsaken. Our records must be on high for it has our witness contained therein.

THE BUILT UP SOUL

Our lives is not our own; they belong to God. God has made promises not to us alone but to nations. In the lineage of Jesus Christ we do away with the nastiness of the flesh and spirit. We don't turn our eyes when sin is before us but we do something about it.

Christians turn the other cheek in spite of what they believe but yet don't understand. The Devil is a liar and the accuser of the brethren; he causes man through lies and trickery to sin, then accuse us to God. But thanks be unto Jesus that He is the deliverer of the captives and sets them free. Never forget how we were made free from sin!

Put yourself aside for the Kingdom and its works. Be a part of God's divine plan and mandate, submit to the Holy Spirit. Jesus has already overcome and it's time we be about the footwork of Christ. Satan is an enemy to the world and he wants a kingdom, don't allow him to build his kingdom in us.

We at all times must maintain our virtue by holding on to the office we are called to and keeping a virtuous heart toward God. We must put away from us everything not like God. We must deny Satan in every area of our life. We must stay the course of this life with Christ God's Way.

Hatred is as malignant as the worst kind of cancer. Discord and discontent is as lethal as the poison that comes from a venomous snake. The venom will kill with the one whip of the snakes tongue. It is as malicious and vicious as a lion and so antagonistic that no one can penetrate their psyche to bring them out of the virile effect of that state.

They must come to Christ and repent that they once again become vibrant and a strong force against the enemy that has come to rob us of our souls.

Man is not our enemy, the Devil is. We need God to help us to be vigilant that we can be watchful, alert, observant, and attentive to the spirit that can take control of us that will turn us away from God. It's time to wake up America; awake out of sleep and observe to do all that is required of us in Christ and out of Christ.

When it comes to Christ we need 20/20 vision that cast out all vices that comes our way. Vices are wickedness, corruption, evil, depravity, immorality, iniquity or malignancy.

We have substituted things for God, delegated the works of our calling to entities that God didn't ordain. A virtuous heart after God will not breach, infringe, transgress or trespass the Laws of God or the Law of the Land in which we live.

A virtuous heart grows in Christ and acquire the right affection not only for God but the whole of mankind. A virtuous heart when acquired decides its time to take our minds off of man and set our affections on things above, not on things of the earth. We must love God more than our own selves that we dismiss the foolishness of high mindedness and become humble to what we know is right to do.

Submit to God today, hear what God is saying; be not conformed to this world but be transformed by the renewing of your minds. We must think about edifying our soul rather than our pocketbooks. The love of money is the root of all evil. It's a driving force that will take one to hell. We have one foot on earth and one in hell. It's time to examine ourselves whether we be in Christ, for God or not.

THE BUILT UP SOUL

The Soul That Sin

I John 3:9 whosoever is born of God doth not commit sin, for his seed remaineth in Him and he cannot sin because he is born of God.

All unrighteousness is sin *1 John 5:*17. God makes known to us our sin which now makes us accountable for our doings and acts. We must hear and know God's Word concerning our lives. We must confess and acknowledge our sins. *Psalm 38:18* David said for I will declare my iniquity, I will be sorry for my sin. Our sin is constantly before us.

The soul that sin shall die as is what happened with Adam and Eve. Come let us reason together God said (*Isaiah 1:18*) though your sins be as scarlet they shall be as white as snow, thou they be red like crimson, they shall be as wool. God will blot out our transgressions for his own sake. We need to continue to seek Him even in our messed up state.

Unbelief is sin and bullying is as bad. Who really is the unbelieving? Who really is setting bad examples? Lying sets off a spirit of deception. Disrespect being loosed sets off hatred. WOW, sounds like Satan landed in the life of man and he doesn't care if we are black or white, brown, blue, green, or gold; He is desperate for our soul.

He wants our soul fool! We are doing exactly as he has planned to put us on our way to hell along with the people whose soul we have infected with hatred, envy, jealousy, and lying. All sin to the Spirit of God. Yes people of all race and ethnic origins in have sin issues but they aren't stupid!

Lying is a sin; it is a breaking of the Commandment "thou shalt not lie". Which is worse? The Devil is the father of lies; so if we too stoop to lies and deceit you are a servant of the Devil. Why should we be trusted? It's time to repent. We are servants of God who voluntarily dedicates our self to the service of God that learns to stay repentant.

Who are the people we are trying to please? We sell the devil our soul for a minute but thank God Satan didn't do what he wanted to do in that minute that could have taken us out of this world. He is self-destructing himself; he would never be forgiven.

We all have stooped to lies that men fed us and too was deceived even by loved ones; God! God knows those that are with us. Leave the pundants alone and take care of the business we have been hired by God to do! Now if God hired us; He can fire us too! Repentance and remission of sin should be taught in Jesus Name among all nations.

Keep not fighting amongst yourselves. God will expose man's sin for the world to see if when we repent the sin and quit it.. God will show himself Mighty. Deception brings dishonor to God. It destroys the fruits of the ground we stand upon; truth.

We are to be a delightsome land but our own words has been stout against us; the very fiber of one being undivided with God and man. We are so divided we don't know what we have said or didn't say. We talk more against each other than the enemy does. We are losing ground with others because we are so disrespectful to God.

Division, division, division! Division is a spirit of sin. God is sick of division. Satan was kicked out of heaven along with all those that followed his leading and is chained up already judged but awaiting punishment for their betrayal. God sees that He will have to punish some people for their constant rebelliousness to Him. This position we take in Christ is no natural appointment. It is concerning the people and their acts toward God.

God knows how to clean up this world; He created it. All of the egotistically moved people that say they love God but lie, lie, lie will be punished for their acts. Lives are at stake and men will lift their eyes in Hell. Hell is real, yes it is. It's a place of punishment for sinners.

It was originally created for the Devil and those disobedient angels that followed him in his takeover try for heaven. He wants to give us a free pass to hell too! Keep on thinking that it is not real. The Devil is a liar and God will destroy all those that fight against the prick; Him.

Just know that if we fight the leadership of this world, we are not fighting a man, we are fighting God. America is the land of the free; a promised land for all people, every race, every color, and every ethnicity. America represents something!

Step back boys and pull your pants up; take your lick. The youth is the leaders of today not tomorrow. The youth have visions, old men dream dreams. It's time to retire the dreams and let the visions come forth.

God called the Church to deal with the sin issue. He called Kings {leaders} to lead the nations, not play marbles like little boys, deal with the business at hand legislating and executing the law of that land. He had Judges in the Bible that judged the breakers of the law.

THE BUILT UP SOUL

We are making God sick. Not only is He sick of our rhetoric, He is sick of our lies. Repent now or die a bastard; it's your choice. For what profit is there to gain the whole world and lose your own soul?

Big In whose eyesight? A big man, a big woman; is big in whose eyesight? Some people look big and are not really as big as some think. Steroids blow some people up and without muscle its just fat; unwanted fat. No one wants to be fat, it just happens.

No one really wants to be big; some had a choice and some did not. Skinny today some think is fat. So where are the fat cats when you need them? Where are they hiding? In the Church, in the world or any in between we find that there is contention. Contention is there because somebody doesn't want to obey what God has said.

Somebody is still finding excuse for what they don't want to do. It's time out for the buddy system; it's time to put God's Word to work in our lives. God wants the Word to become big in us; He wants his Word to be big in us and He wants his Word to consume us and we must, I must, you must make it so. It's an individual relationship.

We want man to see us one way, God to see us one way, but God wants us to see Him! He wants to be the only big in our eyesight. Satan is an enemy to the world and he wants a kingdom, don't allow him to build his kingdom in us. We at all times must maintain our virtue holding on to a virtuous heart toward.

Hatred is as malignant as the worst kind of cancer. Discord and discontent is as lethal as the poison that comes from a venomous snake. The venom

THE BUILT UP SOUL

will kill with the one whip of the snakes tongue. It is as malicious and vicious as a lion and so antagonistic that no one can penetrate their psyche to bring them out of the virile effect of that state.

They must come to Christ and repent that they once again become vibrant and a strong force against the enemy that has come to rob us of our souls.

Man is not our enemy, the Devil is. We need God to help us to be vigilant that we can be watchful, alert, observant, and attentive to the spirit that can take control of us; that will not turn us away from God.

It's time to wake up world, awake out of sleep and observe to do all that is required of us in Christ and out of Christ.

THE BUILT UP SOUL

Time For Renewed Relationship

II Corinthians 4:15-18 for all things are for your sakes, that the abundant grace might through the thanksgiving of many redound to the glory of God. For which cause we faint not but though our outward man perish, yet the inward man is renewed day by day. For our light afflictions which is but for a moment, worketh for us a far more exceeding and eternal weight of glory; while we look not at the things which are seen, but at the things which are not seen; for the things which are seen are temporal, but the things which are not seen are eternal.

God is saying today that the world is full of junk, junkie parents, junkie kids, and junkie bodies". "Men live junkie lives, use junkie drugs and feed the children junkie foods". I said "what's up God"? He said; I have too many spiritual junkies in my house not doing what they are supposed to be doing in my name and for my sake. I said "okay" and He said they are the "junkiest of junkies".

Well, you ask; what is a junkie? Junkie is the slang for a narcotics peddler or addict; a person who derives inordinate pleasure from or who is dependent on something or a junk dealer. A junkie is one who is characterized as one of poor quality, trash having little meaning worth or significance.

As I began to clean a stove I got from a cousin of mine, I noticed how dirty it was. It had grease packed up on top of it, under the top part of it, down the sides and front and on the overhead. I said God! I needed a stove and was glad he gave it to me but I said "God how could he keep something this dirty in his house or cook on it like this and eat the food"? I looked at the burners and the drainers

80

THE BUILT UP SOUL

and they were wrapped in aluminum foil. When I went to clean them I found that the foil had been wrapped over dirt, grease and scum; not once but two or three times. God! God said "when your life is not clean and pure you don't care what you do or surround yourself with".

It took me four hours to clean that stove top to bottom. Now it looks like it's a little new, it took some time and work but I have a stove to my liking.

God wants us to clean up our lives. Deliverance is a process and isn't complete until the day we stand before God; the race is not to the swift nor the strong but to them that endure until the end. Jesus said in *Matthew 24:13* but he that shall endure unto the end, the same shall be saved. Why did He say this? He said it because of the day we live in right now.

Jesus spoke of man's destruction of his temple and the Temple of God because of the antecedent calamities man would face in the last days. We are to take heed that no man deceive us, for many come in the name of the Lord but their agenda reaches not the heart of God. We shall hear of wars and rumors of war and nation shall rise against nations and kingdom against kingdom, there shall be famines, and pestilences, and earthquakes in divers places.

All of these things are the beginning of sorrows and we shall be delivered up to be afflicted. Why are we asleep in God's house? Why aren't we rendering unto God fervent effectual prayers? Why is it that; man's heart is failing God every day? We the people of God have become spiritual junkies. We are guilty of what Jesus said in *Matthew 6:33-34* concerning seeking the kingdom of God. We don't

81

THE BUILT UP SOUL

want to make any sacrifices to do the work of God which is kingdom building, ridding the junk out of the life of man in the earth that we all are ready to receive the heavenly reward of promise; eternal life.

Once man make Christ their personal savior, they need help and guidance through the Word that will work on purifying their life to be more like Christ. Well every situation we find our self in, God speaks to us concerning life and getting the junk out of our lives. He deal with us personally concerning how He feels concerning us and the sacrifices he makes for us all the time that we too doesn't deserve.

That's how it is with God. It takes time to make Saints. We ought to get tired of the junk and mess we entangle ourselves into. Cleanliness is Godliness; it's not next to it. Sacrifices are made every day even through the struggle of whether we deserve it or not.

Many say they love God but lives an abominable lifestyle. This life was as dirty in God's sight as that stove was in mine. The filth just built up and the dirt and grime of his life also was built up in filth on the stove, in the stove and around the stove. This is a comparison to how we just pile sin up in our lives. It compares to the fact that we try to hide sin again and again.

When we live a life of sin we will lie again and again and again to stay ahead of the game. We will steal whatever it is that we want to make us look the part of what we are trying to live, in and out of God. We will cheat, beat, and eat away at anyone that gets in our way and cover it up. When a man will do these things in his life he is his own worst enemy. He is full of junk and it is the junkiest times of his life rather they know it or not.

THE BUILT UP SOUL

We pad sin like we are covering up a surgical wound. We put salve on the wound and cover it up with a bandage but it's not being cleaned. We are fleshly junkies to sin because we live to please the appetites of the flesh rather than the Lord. The junkiest mess of a man's life is their own natural ability to fulfill the desires of their own lust.

The love of God has waxed cold in the lives of many Christians today. Jesus warns us in **Matthew 24:12** that the love of many shall wax cold. It's all about me and mine. What I have man say; I caused it to come to past. We seek for things not eternal in the kingdom of God. Jesus said to seek ye first the kingdom of God and his righteousness and all these things shall be added unto you.

We take so much time thinking on somethings when Jesus said to take no thought for the morrow for the morrow shall take thought for the things of itself. Sufficient to the day is the evil thereof. We are laying up treasures that are not well pleasing to God. The treasure we are to lay is the Word of God and everything else will take and line itself up.

The paper on the floor represents the way we treat God's earth; we trash it. The dirt, grime, and grease on the stove represent stuff we get and waste every day because we don't need it. The sacrifices we should make to our fellow man are not there; we only care about ourselves. We are spiritual junkies because the way that we take seem right to man but the end thereof are the ways of death.

We are too pleasing to man but not God. We seek the notoriety of man but it's not to bring glory to God as we pretend. The fact is we get a high off of being high. To be high minded is the mind of the people that went against Jesus in the earth. All of the stuff that is covered up in the spiritual will be brought to the forefront; be sure our sin will find us out and embarrass us too.

Spiritual junkies use their positions to get what they want and God is an after-thought. It's time in this season to reconsider our ways. It's time to really be thankful that God hasn't destroyed us in our doings. Church after Church and people supposedly be of God has been exposed of deeds done in the dark and God is not through.

If we want exposure let it be of sincerity and faithfulness toward God. Let us not faint in the Ministry to which we have been called. Let us renounce the hidden things of dishonesty, not walk in craftiness, nor handle the Word of God deceitfully; but be manifestation of the truth commending ourselves to every man's conscience in the sight of God.

If our gospel be hid, it is hid to them that are lost to them that the god of this world has blinded the minds because they believe not. Jesus called us to reprove the world of sin; we are to bring the light to the glorious gospel of Christ, who is the image of God which we pattern ourselves after.

Don't just get the gospel and hide behind it for our image to be brought forth; for then we become spiritual junkies. We are building a high place off of someone else's work. We preach not ourselves but Christ Jesus the Lord; and that we are his servants only.

It is God who commanded the light to shine out of darkness, out of the mess we have made of our lives, out of the dirt and grime we have hid in our closets, out of the greased up lies we have told, out

THE BUILT UP SOUL

of the things we have stolen, out of the total disrespect we have one for another, and out of the dishonest approach we make toward Him. It is God that have saved us from the same destruction and judgment He has already placed on Satan and all the fallen angels with him.

God wants to shine in our hearts and give us the knowledge of the glory of God in the face of Jesus Christ. He brings us this knowledge because he wants us to get the junk out of our lives. He don't want us to be rejected because of ignorance and wickedness in our hearts. We have treasure in earthen vessels that the excellency of the power may be of God and not us.

We are troubled on every side, perplexed but not in despair; persecuted but not forsaken; cast down, but not destroyed; always bearing about in the body the dying of the Lord Jesus that the life also of Jesus might be made manifest in our mortal body. Although for his sake we are always being delivered unto death take it for it is the life that will come forth to save the lost.

We are to press in the way and realize that what's important will come to the forefront of all we go through. We are to have the same Spirit of faith which Jesus possessed. We are to trust God that He knows how to raise up the lost and us.

Let's be thankful unto the Lord and bless His name. We don't physically see Him but we believe that He is Lord and that Hge is the rewarder of life to man that call upon His name. We should give thanks to God for sending His son in the likeness of sinful flesh to redeem us from ourselves that we may get in right relationship with Him again.

85

THE BUILT UP SOUL

We, you and I don't want to be spiritual junkies, they are the junkiest junkies in the world. Be like Jesus. Let's get right Church and let's go home. These built buildings will be left here in the earth, but these fleshly buildings got to get up out of here; for that which God created will return to Him!

What are we going to do when the trumpet sound on our life as we know it? Will we be ready to cross over and go through the gate to heaven? God is standing there and our life will be read off; what will be written of you? Of me?

The gifts and calling of God is without repentance. we learn God through life challenges. when we stand to preach the Word it is God standing; we are in His stead allowing Him to speak through us. We are most effective in preaching during our challenges because they are so real and alive. The challenge helps us to understand God and learn as well as teach.

THE BUILT UP SOUL

We Have Heard, Now Do

Galatians 5:16-17 this I say then, walk in the Spirit and you shall not fulfill the lusts of the flesh. For the flesh lusteth against the Spirit and the Sirit against the flesh, and these are contrary the one to the other; so that ye cannot do the things that ye would.

Live The Gospel! Our glance here is a look at our lives, not only being a testimony, but also producing God's fruit in the lives of others after Christ Jesus. How do we do that; by how we ourselves manufacture God's fruit in the earth by how we ourselves live.

If we are to stay alive in Christ our conversion comes with some do's and don'ts. The Word of God is not just to hear; but to do it. Our lives must line up to the Word. We are living now to live again with Christ when He returns.

We have at some point in life heard the gospel now its time to do it right in our life. It's not enough just to read them off the page, but we have to live with the fruit of the Spirit alive in us. We show the love of God to all men by living truthfully the gospel of Christ Jesus.

Take note that our body is styled in the form of a tree; so where did the ape come from? Heir is a teaching in science that man came and was evolved from an ape; God forbid they denounce God and his Creation for a lie from Satan. A tree started with a seed, it takes root, it has a trunk, and then branches, and it produces fruit. Just like a tree we are styled in like manner.

We are a seed that takes root and grow into a body, branches of arms and legs and we produce fruit. For that fruit to develop and mature, we also must nurture it. We must water it and give it the right amount of fertilizer, so as our spiritual fruit, they must be nurtured with the study of the Word, prayer, fasting, and a submitted conscience of the fruit of the Spirit.

Galatians 5:19-21 lists very clearly the works of the flesh, while *Galatians 5:22-23* lists the fruit of the Spirit. In reading this text we find that the works of the flesh far out number the fruit of the Spirit. In exhibiting these fruit, we want to always be mindful to have the same mind one toward another, minding not high things but condescending to men of low estate.

People our foundation must be sure. The word fruit is significant for three reasons. It means the result, the product, the outcome, or effect produced in the believer's life. Unlike the gifts of the Spirit, every Christian must possess the fruit of the Spirit.

God gives the gifts of the Spirit to each individual differently. Everybody doesn't possess the Gifts of the Spirit but every Christian must possess the fruit of the spirit in their lives.

In *Galatians 5:19-21* the fruits of the flesh are listed. Every person born in this world is capable of performing those fruits of the flesh because they aren't learned, but we were born in sin and shaped in iniquity. But only God gives his Spirit and his fruit comes only through God producing them in our lives.

Our Christian character is a result of Christ living in us. Christians have to let God develop character in them. Our fertilizer consists of prayer, the prayer that we offer up daily, the reading of the Word everyday and being submitted to God in every area of life. We have to guard our heart and mind. Our heart and mind are the blossoming fruit of the tree.

If we don't watch out, someone will steal us off of our tree, eat us up, and spit us out. That's all our fruit will be, waste. Satan sets out to destroy everything godly in the life of man. We have to guard the fruit entrusted into our care, we have to watch over them, and we have to protect them, prevent entrance and exit of certain things.

The fruit of the Spirit is put on trial when we have confessed to have them in our life, get ready to go through the test. We need a guard to stand watch in the house of where the Spirit dwells to protect the fruit and that house, that tree is our body. We have to be rooted and grounded in the truth that the fruit of the Spirit will be productive in our lives.

Hang out with folks that reverence God. It's more costly to be Spirit minded than to live in the flesh, but it's our job to crucify the flesh anyway so we don't mind giving it up. Don't you know that we are more Spirit than flesh, and if we only feed the flesh, then the Spirit is dying daily?

We have to feed the Spirit of God in us that we may have his fruit growing in our lives every day. We have to live the gospel.

Romans 8:7 tells us that the carnal mind is enmity against God and not subject to the law, the spirit and the flesh have mutual dislike of each other. The Spirit hates the flesh and the flesh hates the Spirit. So we can't yield to both. We have to yield to one or the other and to grow spiritually means to die to the flesh.

They that are after the Spirit, mind the things of the Spirit and they that are after the flesh mind the

THE BUILT UP SOUL

things of the flesh. If we keep it in our mind that I am going to be mean and ugly instead of being kind and good, then we will be mean and ugly. We cannot even please God in the flesh. We owe nobody anything but God, for God sent his son and his son paid it all. He paid it all for us; me and you.

When the fruit of the Spirit is alive in our life, we don't mind making an offering of sacrifice to God. Now an offering is the act of presenting something acceptable unto a worthy receptacle. We can't make an offering of something we don't want our self. We don't mind going where God says to go.

We are showing forth the fruit that is exhibited in our life and we do what he says we are to do. We don't take the wrong folks with us when we go. They may stop us from doing what God says do. We've got to be careful about where we go and whom we take with us.

God seeks for and wants our offering that brings glory to Him. He wants an offering of thanksgiving, our offering of praise, our **offering of sacrifice, giving up wh**at we love most.

He wants us to be submitted, giving up everything, our offering of submission. He wants us to give him an offering through total surrendering. Lose the reign of our life and let God, build an altar, and get in the presence of God, stay close to God and flow with your purpose. Let's stay within the realm of self-control or temperance.

God's Spirit gives us control. If God has given us control through his Spirit, why let somebody or something else drive you. They will change your nature, and instead of being kind, you'll be mean, instead of being gentle, being considerate, kind, patient, not harsh, severe or violent, but managing these through gentleness and after these our moral excellence, will make us socially correct, proper and able to be counted on through our goodness. Why let somebody kill our fruits, why let somebody steal our fruit after God, why let somebody cause our fruit to be rotten, a tree that's planted and rooted in Christ.

Jesus can only produce the fruit that God has already placed in our heart. Just work on good fruit; work on the fruit that edify God. Work on those things that God would be glorified in. Offer him that praise of worship, worshipping him in a Spirit of praise. Kill that old mean and ugly spirit within us that the world offers for our detriment.

Worshipping and praising Him will bring us to a state of submission, a state of sweetness, a state of tenderness, a state of obedience, it will help us to have some self control, to be in control of those old lusts, those things that we go after that's not godly, whatever the eye see, we want, whatever the body feel, we give it to it.

Then there is that old spirit of pride that keeps us puffed up, can't nobody tell us anything. The Devil is a lie. Live the Gospel. Be not conformed to this world, but be ye transformed by the renewing of your mind that ye might prove what is that good and perfect and acceptable will of God (**Romans 12:2**). Our main goal should be to challenge the pattern of the world through our committed life in Christ.

Romans 12:10 tells us to be kindly affectionate one to another with brotherly love in honor, preferring one another, to be of the same mind one towards another. Mind not high things but condescend to men of low estate, be not wise in your own conceits, those thought, those ideas, those opinions; conceits is one's too high opinion of one's ability, their worth or personality. As the mind is changed and renewed through Bible Study, Prayer, Fasting and Fellowship with other believers, our life transforms to be like Jesus.

Romans 12:18 tell us that as much as be possible that lies in us, live peaceably with all men. We have to be different we have to make the difference. We dare to differ. One thing that sets us as believers apart for God's service, occurs when the believer stops conforming to the world!

We are to not be conformed to this world, but hear and do live the gospel of Jesus Christ that rules in our life everyday. Perform to fulfill our purpose of bringing glory to God everyday. We must let gentleness show forth in our life, let kindness show forth in our life, let temperance or self control show forth in our life.

Somebody should see God through the fruit that is amplified in our life each and everyday. Don't just be in the Gospel in word only, but live the Gospel. We have heard; now do! The godly inspired word comes by God, through revelation knowledge, Christian experience, bumps, bruises, hurts and pains and through chastening of the Lord.

God sent the Word that we may inspire someone else to not only confess and profess Christ with their mouth, but through true heartfelt love for Christ, by how well we obey his Word and must first learn how to obey God's Holy Word, follow the leading of the Holy Ghost, and love with the agape love of God. For God is love. He gave his only begotten son to redeem mankind back to Him. We are a token to mankind of God's love. We have a testimony because God loves us, he is ever merciful and open to our needs. For he said in his Word, **Philippians 4:19**, but my God shall supply all of our need according to his riches and glory through Christ Jesus.

Man looks at our past and tries to hold us there, in the past. It seems that what a person see and hear is ever in their minds, so that they won't let go of it. You see we have a choice. Sin is a choice we choose. We choose to sin and sin takes us down a street sometime of no return. In Hell you will lift up your eyes.

For what profit is there in sin? None, nothing but destruction. They can't see what God wants to do in you, until God catches our good up with the bad. We are to have a desire for that which will set the focus on our own life, call into repentance those things that will separate us from God, and walk down that straight and narrow path that will cause us to hear and do the Word.

We must live God's Gospel in a way that will cause us to flow, edify God and be that walking epistle that everyone needs to see us as. We are the only Bible that some people will see or read. The Bible in **I Corinthians 9:14**, it says, even so hath the Lord ordained that they which preach the gospel should live of the gospel.

The Gospel is not to the praise of God's glory, but we are and we should live the gospel that we preach. Our life is the only Bible some people will ever read. Where will our reward be if we go contrary to the Word? We should live the gospel so that we may obtain others in the gospel. We have to keep under subjection our body individually!

THE BUILT UP SOUL

Life Altering Changes

There are things that can happen in our life that can ultimately take us out of this world if we don't keep our mind together

Divorce – Separation and children

Death – Tragically and naturally- to husband, wife and children

Loss of job – Income – What it means to the family

Loss of love and support

Loss of possession – Sentimental value

Loss of covering – walking out of the will of God

In these things we will find out if we love the Lord or not, will we continue in Him, We will find out where we are placing our trust. In adversity we should trust God more and think less. In *I Kings 19:1-10* we find that after we have had our greatest victory, because we are tired, our flesh is weak; we are open to attack from the enemy.

Being accused – being a suspect in something you know nothing about or even had anything to do with it.

Being lied on – a liar that won't quit – people will lie on us for their own personal reasons or gain.

Deception – we will find out who is really who, when they think we are being blessed. He who laughs at you will not be laughing in the end.

Pure love is undefiled – coming through the storm – it's not what you go through, but how you come out. Keep the faith; trust God and he will work it out to our good. We can survive in the midst of problems, circumstances, and situations. The storm is over!

II Corinthians 4:15-18 for all things are for your sakes, that the abundant grace might through the thanksgiving of many redound to the glory of God. For which cause we faint not but though our outward man perish, yet the inward man is renewed day by day. For our light afflictions which is but for a moment, worketh for us a far more exceeding and eternal weight of glory; while we look not at the things which are seen, but at the things which are not seen; for the things which are seen are temporal, but the things which are not seen are eternal.

Consider me says the Lord, why not? We give consideration to every thing in the world, but what about God that created and made us? Job was special in that he trusted God for all things. We learn that through the experience he had with God, Satan, and man was a lesson learned for all of us.

When we consider the pain and agony he faced from his friends, neighbors and others that just did not understand what he was going through we understand his wife's stand that he should curse God and die. How many of us curse God and die at the first onset of trouble? She didn't consider that Job served God not for the things that he lost during this time but because Job actually loved God that he would obey Him even in death.

As we go through life we will find out what true and real forgiveness is all about. When Jesus told us in the model prayer to us in *Matthew 6:9-13* he carried forgiveness a little farther afterwards in verses *14-15*. We are to forgive others their thoughts, actions, and doings against us and against God. We must forgive those that sin against us and those that sin against God. Because they don't personally do something to us don't mean that they haven't sinned.

The world needs forgiveness. Consider me, why not Lord, use my mouth to ask for the forgiveness of the natural family that has mistreated us? Consider me, why not Lord, use my mouth to ask for the forgiveness of the spiritual family that has mistreated God? God did say we have a responsibility to the whole of the world. We are all family of one body and that is the body of Christ.

Our witness is on high, our record is on high; what have we done for Christ? Have we considered doing more for Him as He has done for us? Our lives is not our own; we belong to God. Thanks for His love. Down at the altar is where we are to pray, it's at the altar a spiritual change is made.

The Father, the Word, and the Spirit they all agree; they all bear record in earth. It's true; down at the altar, down on our knees we make a difference in this world. We need a more personal relationship with Christ that is not just in the Church house; we need to become the Church of Jesus Christ in our heart, mind, body, soul, and spirit.

We need the heart of God, the mind of Christ, a body that obeys the Word, a soul that will live for eternity and a spirit that follows the Holy Spirit's lead from earth back to glory no matter what we go through in this life.

We are one in Christ, one with God, and one in Spirit and it's time to realize that we are our brother's keeper. How many times must we forgive? According to Jesus seventy times seventy;

that's a life time of forgiveness. We wish that all could be free as Jesus was but all will not be free. In **St. John 8:32** Jesus said and ye shall know the truth and the truth shall make you free.

We so many times refuse the truth; don't want to accept the truth so how can we be free? Father forgive; us our trespasses and forgive those that trespass against us whether it is be in deed or word.

When we fast we need to consider our ways. Do we fast for men or for nought? Many prayers are prayed with impure motives and intents. Many are prayed not from the innermost being where some intimacy with God is involved, in secret or in private but out in the open before men to be heard or seen.

Consider our ways we aren't as innocent as we pretend. There is no honesty connected with us and God. It's time to consider me; see if I am pure in my thoughts, unblemished in my actions, wholesome in my lifestyle, upright in my dealings with others, righteous before God and true to Christ. Life altering changes makes us consider God.

Ask God, am I the cause of men dying in sin? Am I guiltless of their sin? Are we that naïve that we think we aren't the cause of much that goes on? Well we are not; consider me. We need some new innovation in our lives; some change, some newness, and some addition where Christ come in and the Spirit leads.

There are many life altering changes we face. We are not free from hurt, and afflictions but we are also not free from causing these either. Consider me, contemplate, regard, think, and believe that what is important to you is important to God also. So why not make what is important to Him a part of our resume? What is important to God is far more important to us then we think for this is our salvation and redemption to eternal life.

Giving ourselves to the Word is of noteworthy importance; it is significant. Giving of our abundance to the use of God is substantial. When we kindly consider God in our thoughts, acts, and doings we are giving attention to eternal life. This is the life that Jesus gained for us in the redemption process to make the payment for sin on man's behalf.

What has happened to men that they don't want to be servants anymore, but Fathers? There are many fathers but only one Father and that's God Himself. There are those that go about killing the body of Christ unaware and souls are at stake. Men take matters into their own hands aborting the promises of God. They make life altering decisions based on their own intellect rather than consult God!

We lean to our own understanding but God works against the grain of our thinking. We are not able to rely on our thoughts; our thoughts are after material things and we are never satisfied. We can accomplish things on this side of life as sinners. But to accomplish spiritual things in this life we need God's Word and Spirit that causes change in us that moves us from the natural to the Spiritual.

Without us changing us there will be no Spiritual resurrection. We were first spiritual, then natural. God created man a spirit being in his image male and female then he made man a body from the dust of the earth and separated the two and called them man and woman. Instructions were given to

THE BUILT UP SOUL

them as spirit beings in the Creation and were to be followed and manifested in the made humans. The Spiritual being had no problem obeying, it was not until flesh was added and they were separated. In oneness is power; consider me says the Lord.

Men's accomplishment includes but is not limited to the things we can bring about to completion; but those that God make happen in our lives. It is God that gives men visions and provision to work the vision. Many men have succeeded in reaching the goals they set for ministry while others struggle. Does that mean they are better men? No.

Should we look upon them as to what has been accomplished? We have a more crucial goal to meet and that's to stand before God in holiness and righteousness and answer the call when it is made. God forgives men their sin but there is judgment that comes with that sin. The sin we are talking about today is the spirit of pride; the pride of life!

Man has forgotten to consider that it is the Lord that has done these things and not we ourselves. Father forgive my family, forgive my church family, forgive me my transgressions and iniquities, forgive my brothers and sisters, forgive my co-workers, forgive those that sin against me, and forgive all those that sin against my Father known and unknown.

Satan is an enemy to the world and he wants a kingdom, don't allow him to build his kingdom in us. We at all times must maintain our virtue holding on to a virtuous heart toward God. Life changing situations do occur; but God is stiil in control, consider Him in all we do.

THE BUILT UP SOUL

Hatred is as malignant as the worst kind of cancer. Discord and discontent is as lethal as the poison that comes from a venomous snake. The venom will kill with the one whip of the snakes tongue. It is as malicious and vicious as a lion and so antagonistic that no one can penetrate their psyche to bring them out of the virile effect of that state.

We must come to Christ and repent that they once again become vibrant and a strong force against the enemy that has come to rob us of our souls.

Man is not our enemy, the Devil is. We need God to help us to be vigilant that we can be watchful, alert, observant, and attentive to the spirit that can take control of us that will turn us away from God. It's time for all men to wake up; awake out of sleep and observe to do all that is required of us in Christ and out of Christ.

When it comes to Christ we need 20/20 vision that cast out all vices that comes our way. Vices are wickedness, corruption, evil, depravity, immorality, iniquity or malignancy. We have substituted things for God, delegated the works of our calling to entities that God didn't ordain.

A virtuous heart after God will not breach, infringe, transgress or trespass the Laws of God or the Law of the Land in which we live no matter the life changing circumstance presented us. A virtuous heart grows in Christ and acquire the right affection not only for God but the whole of mankind.

A virtuous heart when acquired decides its time to take our minds off of man and set our affections on things above, not on things of the earth. We must

THE BUILT UP SOUL

love God more than our own selves that we dismiss the foolishness of high mindedness and become humble to what we know is right to do.

Submit to God today, hear what God is saying; be not conformed to this world but be transformed by the renewing of your minds. We must think about edifying our soul rather than our pocketbooks.

The love of money is the root of all evil. It's a driving force that will take one to hell.

We have one foot on earth and one in hell. It's time to examine ourselves whether we be in Christ, for God or not

God has an issue with us, it's not about us in this earth but a man believing and trusting in the Almighty God. Unbelief is sin and bullying is as bad. Who really is the unbelieving? Who really is setting bad examples? Lying sets off a spirit of deception. Disrespect being loosed sets off hatred.

Satan landed in the earth from heaven and he doesn't care if we are black or white, brown, blue, green, or gold. He wants our soul; don't be fooled. We are doing exactly as he has planned to put us on our way to hell along with the people whose soul has been infected with hatred, envy, jealousy, and lying. All sin to the Spirit of God.

Yes people of all race and ethnic have sin issues but they aren't stupid! Lying is a sin; it is a breaking of the Commandment "thou shalt not lie". Which is worse? The Devil is the father of lies; so if we will stoop to lies and deceit we are a servant of the Devil. Why should we then be trusted? It's time to repent. Many times Satan didn't do what he wanted to do to us that was to take us out of this world; he is self-destructing himself where he would never be forgiven. He want man to stoop to his lies. God knows those in earth that is for Him and against Him. We too know the truth as to identifying them that is with God and God does too! He is putting the warning out, take heed.

Deception brings dishonor to God. It destroys the fruits of the ground we stand upon; truth. This world right now is not a delightsome land. Our own words has been stout against us; the very fiber of one being divided. We are so divided we don't know what we have said or didn't say.

We talk more against each other than the enemy does. We are losing ground with God because we are so disrespectful to the Word of God; for we will not obey what He says therein. Division, division, division! God is sick of division. The spirit of confusion and division is has no part of God's makeup.

Satan was kicked out of heaven along with all those that followed his leading and is chained up already judged but awaiting punishment for their betrayal. God sees that He will have to punish some people for their constant rebelliousness to a leader that was already ordained for the position he presides in; both spiritually and naturally.

The earth is the Lord's and the fullness thereof; the world and they that dwell therein, *Psalm 24:1*. God knows how to clean up this world; He created it. All of the egotistically moved people that say they love

THE BUILT UP SOUL

God but lie, lie, lie will be punished for their acts. Lives are at stake and men will lift their eyes in Hell. Hell is real, yes it is. It's a place of punishment for sinners.

It was originally created for the Devil and those disobedient angels that followed him in his takeover try for heaven. He wants to give us a free pass to hell too! Keep on thinking that it is not real.

The Devil is a liar and God will destroy all those that fight against the prick; Him.

God called the Church to deal with the sin issue. He called Kings {leaders} to lead the nations, not play marbles like little boys, deal with the business at hand legislating and executing the law of that land. He had Judges in the Bible that judged the breakers of the law.

We are making God sick. Not only is He sick of our rhetoric, He is sick of our lies. Repent now or die a bastard; it's your choice. For what profit is there to gain the whole world and lose our own soul?

Big In Whose Eyesight, A big man, a big woman; is big in whose eyesight? Some people look big and are not really as big as some think. Steroids blow some people up and without muscle its just fat; unwanted fat. No one wants to be fat, it just happens. No one really wants to be big; some had a choice and some did not.

In the Church, in the world or any in between we find that there is contention. Contention is there because somebody doesn't want to obey what God has said. Somebody is still finding excuse for what they don't want to do. It's time out for the buddy system; it's time to put God's Word to work in our lives.

God wants the Word to become big in us; He wants his Word to be big in us and He wants his Word to consume us and we must, I must, you must make it so.

It's an individual relationship. We want man to see us one way, God to see us one way, but God wants us to see Him! He wants to be the only big in our eyesight.

THE BUILT UP SOUL

Impudent Face

This is a face one puts on when they refuses to come to Christ with a repentant heart. I refuse to carry such a face. In all that I have been through in life I choose to forgive and love God. Many in the face of abuse will boldly say I love what I am doing and will not stop.

Impudent means we are shameless (having or showing no feeling of shame, modesty or decency), immodest (not shy or humble, bold, forward) disrespectful (discourteous, impolite, or rude), and insolent (boldly disrespectful in speech or behavior, arrogantly contemptuous; overbearing, proud).

We are saucy (rude) in our ways. The person that wears this face has no connection with a given matter that is relevant and shows no respect to anything or anyone that matters. We live an inappropriate life that is not suitable to life itself. We will say anything for we are forward in our speech and actions that are disrespectful and oversteps the bounds of propriety or courtesy.

This face is the face of one that lives a shameless and brazen impertinence; defiant to all that matters in life and God. Disrespectful we are and display openly insulting and contemptuous speech and behavior that is flip and provocative levity toward one to whom respect should be shown.

This is the face of the world today in which we live. Accept God builds a house it is good for nothing but to be cast down. In the world in which we live we are subjected to many unpleasant and awkward situations because we have not become shame enough of what is going on around us. We are too acceptable of sin.

When we the church learn to recognize who we are and realize that we have a vital part to play in what is acceptable in this world we will go to the throne of Grace as we should. Just the very thought of any lifestyles not ordained of God; should make us sick.

This face the world is walking around with is wrecking-havoc in the lives of young people everywhere. They don't have a chance to grow up because some idiotic adult has lost their mind and perverts the minds of the young. The young people growth is being disrupted daily with the perversion that goes on in this world today. Satan seeks to cut man off from even coming to know God at all.

With the stuff that is happening to children today why would they think that a God exists? We have to protect our children, grandchildren and the generations to come. It's time to wake up Church; be real, we don't smell the sweet aroma of the Holy Spirit but a stench of sin in the air everywhere.

Sin stinks up the world and all that live in it. We don't have to be accepting when it comes to what we know to be wrong. For what price are we selling out our souls?

This impudent face is a face worn by one that is impenitent; without regret, shame or remorse, unrepentant. They only allow the Word of God to pass through their hearing refusing to turn away from sin.

Peace offerings are passed on to us to keep our mouths shut concerning the things that go on in the world. Are we really that deceived? What affects one affect all; what Adam did all of those thousands of years ago affect us still today. By one man's disobedience sin came into the world and by one man's obedience sin has to depart.

Adam came into the world created a spirit being, male and female. He was then made by the Creator a man of the dust and water of the earth. God made him a body to embody the spirit being created to keep the earth God created. God then saw that he was alone in that everything else that crept upon the earth had a living mate. God then laid Adam down upon the earth and performed the first caesarian in the earth; he took out of man his mate and laid her to his side.

Woman being taken out of man, left him where he no longer had a female part. Why do we sell ourselves short in the earth? We were not made like animals so why do we act like them? We were special made to God's perfection. What a God!

What are we offering back to God for what He has done for us? An offering is that which is offered; specifically that which is presented in divine service; a gift offered with some symbolic intent to a deity, a sacrifice; an oblation.

Offerings to God can be traced from the dawn of human history; vegetable offering (**Gen. 4:3**); sacrifice of the firstling of the flock (**Gen.4:4**); the burnt offering (**Gen. 8:20**), the sacrificial meal (**Gen. 31:54**); and the drink offering (**Gen. 35:14**).

The Law of Moses given to him by God for the people of God regulated the system of offerings to God. Jesus offered up his life that ours may be saved. What are we willing to offer to God?

It takes more than a life; are we willing to give ours that God would be glorified? What a perfect day in life one will have when their total trust is in God! We must meet God diligently. It means that we persevere and is careful in our work, and is industrious.

We seek to do our work for God with careful steady painstaking effort. We esteem God highly with much perseverance; we go through with Him. It means we give a higher degree of attention or care to what we do for God than our own self.

THE BUILT UP SOUL

Only what we do for Christ will last and everything we do for Him must be done as if it is our last time doing it. Nothing should be taken for granted.

What God has done, what Jesus has done, and what the Holy Ghost is doing has been and is considered as true, already settled, requires no special attention and accepted as a matter of course.

We have to get ourselves together to receive of the promise that has already been given and proven.

We have been given by Jesus eternal life. It is the same eternal life man was intended to have when we were created. We were set apart for the purpose of bringing glory to God. This gift was taken from Lucifer, (now Satan) and transferred over to man.

He was the most beautiful angel in heaven that was over the praise and worship. He lost the privilege when he became God's number one enemy and now he is man's number one enemy.

We must understand that Satan is the father of all lies, sin, and deception. He is a spirit that implants himself in the heart and mind of man to steal man's soul and divide God's Kingdom.

We are given to understand this and believe that the Word of God is true. When we seek God with all diligence we seek to know Him. Now that I have come to know God in this more significant way I am positioned to never be abused, talked down to, or feel alone again.

There is now in my life a more perfect day because my face is not impudent; for my eyes is stayed on the prize promised me by Christ! He has given me a reason to live and never give up! Through it all I am encouraged to face life in a more challenging way with the weapons given me to win!

THE BUILT UP SOUL

Fight As A Warrior

When we think about weapons we think of something we can use to fight with. A co-worker of mine was not just in the Army, Navy, Air Force, or Marines but was taught and trained as a Seal. Being a Seal means he was taught, trained, and challenged to be a Weapon. He was developed for War.

There is a war going on in this life we live; both to our physical natural life and spiritual life. We too have to be trained for God's Specific use in His Army. Just as the Seals required more training than the Army or other branches of Military; we as the Army of God requires much training too!

Just as they are trained to kill and destroy everything in sight that is a threat to National Security we are trained and given weapons of mass destruction; God too uses weapons to kill the Devil and his demonic forces.

In Heaven a battle went on for control between God and an angel named Lucifer. Let's just imagine a little bit that Lucifer was the younger brother of God and God was living too long for him to take the throne. Jealousy set in because all of the angels reverence and praise was to God. Lucifer decided he wanted what God had so he developed a spirit of envy and lust. He envied to have the praise, honor and worship everyone gave to God. Deception began!

In my Holy Ghost imagination he laid wait after the worship service to find one weak angel that he could tell something to and draw him away from God. He lied to one of the other angels on God. After this one lie this angel looked for to see what had been perpetrated in his mind by Lucifer.

After seeing what seemed like or looked like might be true, he told another angel. And the story went on around Heaven. How did Lucifer think that God who knows all things would not know what he had done? God sat around and waited to see just how many of his loyal followers would take the bait of that lie.

After a third of the angels had gotten with the lie and followed Lucifer's deception God had Michael the Archangel kick Lucifer and the disobedient angels out of Heaven, changed Lucifer's name to Satan which means adversary, called him the father of lies, and loosed him to run in the world for battle while the disobedient angels is chained up awaiting their sentence in hell. The battle has begun.

God then began his work of Creation. In the beginning was the Word and the Word was God and the Word was with God. God spoke his Word and created the heaven and the earth (**Gen. 1**). Heaven was completely new with all that which was disobedient being kicked out.

God started afresh with his home first and then proceeded with the home he would make for some new souls. As he did, Satan a defeated foe watched to see what would be and what God would say to them. But God took his time, six days to be exact:

1st day: He lightened up the dark world that he may see. He saw that it was good; calling the light day and the darkness night.

2nd day: He made a firmament and divided the waters under the firmament. He called the firmament Heaven. 3rd day: God then gathered the waters under the Heaven together in one place and the dry land He called earth appeared. He called the waters seas. He then spoke that the earth would bring forth grass and herb yielding seed after his kind and fruit of itself after its kind.

4th day: God said let there be lights in the firmament of the heaven to divide the day from the night, let them be for signs and for seasons, days and years. He gave two great lights upon the earth, the greater light (the sun) to

rule the day and the lesser light (the moon) to rule the
night along with stars also. This divided the night from
day and divided the light from the darkness.

5th day: God spoke saying let the waters bring forth
abundantly the moving creatures that hath life and fowl
that may fly above the earth in the open firmament of
heaven. He created the whales and every living creature
that move which the waters brought forth abundantly
after their kind and every winged fowl after his kind. God
blessed them saying be fruitful and multiply, fill the
waters in the seas, and let fowl multiply in the earth.

6th day: Satan finally saw a threat. God said let the earth
bring forth the living creature after his kind, cattle, beasts
and every creeping thing. Then God said let us make
man in our image, after our likeness, and let them have
dominion over everything I have created thus far!

So God created man in his own image, in the image of
God created he him; male and female created he them
(**Gen.1:27**). God blessed them and said to them to be
fruitful and multiply and replenish the earth and subdue it
and have dominion over every living thing that moves
upon the earth.

God provided everything in the earth man would need to
live in the earth before he put us here. He gave us the
herb bearing seed, every tree he gave fruit that would be
for man, meat. To every beast of the earth and every
fowl of the air and to everything that crept upon the earth
that had life he gave the green herb for meat for them to
eat.

Everything was good but even with that Satan was
lurking around waiting on a loophole to dethrone God of
his Creation. How would he get to do that? God seemed
to have everything locked in! As he listened he realized
he had no way in but he wasn't giving up that easy. He
knew that God would reveal something that he would be
able to use against this newly created being he called

man. In my sanctified mind I can see Satan's mind was being filled with questions. He was losing it not knowing what God was up to!

In the life of one that has been abused, we too are always wondering about the change to come and how long will it take God to come and help us. He had been with God in Heaven and could tell that God was up to something; but what?

Satan had waited all these days but he had not heard yet anything that would gain him entrance into the life of man. He wanted to know what was God up to. The challenge was becoming almost too great and he had surely lost.

What was God doing? Why was God resting? God ended his work which he had made; and rested on the seventh day from his work (**Gen. 2:1-3**) and blessed the seventh day, and sanctified it. Why would He need rest, he never needed it before?

Finally on the eighth day God came back with instructions to the man that Satan awaited. **Genesis 2:6-7 but there went up a mist from the earth, and watered the whole face of the ground and the Lord God formed man of the dust of the ground, and breathed into his nostrils the breath of life, and man became a living soul.**

God formed the man finally and put him in the Garden he planted for him. In the midst of the Garden God had planted a tree which he called the tree of life; the tree of knowledge of good and evil (**Gen. 2:9**). God put man in the Garden to dress it and keep it.

Satan is terrified of God showing up for man. When God shows up, the Devil is exposed. All of that was good and fine but what could Satan use against man to make God angry with him? He is listening to hear God speak; for the Word is what he needed to work his dEcEptiOn!

THE BUILT UP SOUL

Here come the instructions (*Gen. 2:16-17*) from God to man. God is speaking so Satan can hear what he is saying; finally! God commanded the man saying, of every tree of the garden thou may freely eat of; but of the tree of the knowledge of good and evil, thou shall not eat of it; for in the day that thou eat thereof thou shall surely die.

Adam and Eve lived in the most perfect of perfect state of all their days upon the earth! All they had to do was obey what God had said. For best results in the life of man even today, is to follow God's instructions and not partake of the tree of sin.

They didn't know that they held the salvation of the whole world in that one test of obedience. How that everything we do affect all those we love. Man's actions still bring forth death in their lives as well as those they love for generations to come.

Here was Satan's entrance to man's exit of that perfect place in Christ; he knew what disobedience was and it's consequences; sin's results. He peeps into the lives of man to see what God is doing even today. This advantage he has over us is because of his prior life in Heaven; he knows the mind and heart of God.

We fail in life because we don't get to know Him as we need to. It's the Word in us that will keep us from falling under attack from the enemy. We need the mind of Christ (*Phil. 2:5*). God's mind is revealed to us in His Word. He uses the Word of God against us. Many as Adam and Eve did have the Word but was deceived by the doubt planted by this fallen foe (*Gen. 3:1-6*).

He knows just what to do to make us disobey and fall from grace. We just haven't realized what's happening yet; that's why we need the Holy Spirit the continuator of the work of Christ in our lives. He is the discerner we need that will lead and guide us through the terrains of life.

THE BUILT UP SOUL

From that day until this one Satan seeks out ways to cause man to disobey God. Now more than ever he realizes that his time is short. He can look even in the earth today and see the wickedness of man and know that Christ is soon to return.

If man gets saved, quit his evil ways of disobedience and tell someone else of God's goodness and mercy, Satan loses ground in his kingdom building efforts. He is no fool, but tries to keep us fooled. How long will we allow his battle with God to keep up out of the Kingdom of Heaven?

We must get busy! Stop allowing Satan to abuse us through these disobedient lifestyles we live. He is on his job, look around us. What do we see? Children are being abused more and more today. They are being lied to and deceived in their search for love. They are finding what they think is love in all the wrong places.

Satan is terrified of God showing up for man. When God shows up, the Devil is exposed. We the people of God must expose the truth of God as it is written. Satan knows that God is honest and perfect in all his doings. He knows that God is just; for God to be dishonest means we are deceived. For all that will sin and live ungodly shall have that same part of the lake with Satan and burn in hell for eternity.

We are deceived liars when we borrow and don't pay back, it can keep us out of heaven, that's stealing. A false balance is an abomination to the Lord and we will be found out just like the thief when he is found out is ashamed. We have to be careful how we build up; lying and stealing is out. God has given us weapons of warfare to ward off this evil foe.

THE BUILT UP SOUL

Taking On The Challenge

Matthew 6:25 therefore I say unto you, take no thought for your life, what ye shall eat or what ye shall drink; nor yet for your body, what ye shall put on. Is not the life more than meat, and the body than raiment? Jesus is asking a question here; why do we give food and clothing more thought than God that has everything?

Is not God able to supply our need without us condescending to the ways of man to get what we desire?

We the people of God is called to a standard that the world must ascend to; not we descend to the world. **Psalm 1:1** David a man after God's heart wrote it like this; blessed is the man that walketh not in the counsel of the ungodly, nor standeth in the way of sinners, nor sitteth in the seat of the scornful.

David had been anointed and appointed by God to do a work for Him in building God's Church. He instead one day sinned a sin that would change his life purpose with God in the world forever. He realized what he had done after God brought it to him by way of the Prophet Nathan in **I Chronicles 17:4**.

The Ark of God remained under the curtains but David dwelled in the best of cedars. Nathan told him what was in his heart but God came and told Nathan what his take on the matter was. You see what we see is man but God see the heart. David's heart was after God but he had also sinned a sin that put blood on his hands which displeased God. Displeasing God will abort God's plan of work in our life.

Sin and disobedience killed God's original plan for man in the earth. God wants an established house. He call all men. He called man from the beginning of all races unto Himself to be unto Him servants of the Lord! It is for our sake, his servants that He do the things for man that he do. We are called as He first sent man to do; fulfill his purpose and his Will in earth as it was done in Heaven.

God had charged David to build him a house to dwell in but David had blood on his hand, for he was a man of prayer but also a man of war. He got crossed up in disobedience and had an innocent man killed to have his wife as his own.

God had sent Nathan the prophet to speak to him concerning the house God had ordained that he build. Now it would be passed down to one in David's lineage.

I Chronicles 17:1-14. Verse *10-14* God told David that He would build him a house of his seed after him and he shall be of his sons; God will establish his kingdom. It would be then that his house shall be built and established forever. God would be his Father and He shall be my Son. God's mercy will dwell with him. He will be settled in this house of the Lord and in God's Kingdom forevermore.

God was talking about Jesus that would build a spiritual house rebuilding the relationship between God and man in the physical house, that inner man; *Hebrews 1:1-5*. Even the angels shall worship him.

This same Jesus established in the earth that which was in the beginning between God and man. God said I will be his Father as He now is ours alike. He took the relationship away with Adam but returned it back to man; whosoever would come back to Him could have that established relationship that they could be the Church that God established.

God wants to be praised and glorified *Ephesians 1:12*; that they should be to the praise of God's Glory, who first trusted in Christ. You see God built his house according to that which He had first spoken unto David; a spiritual house through David seed; Jesus as He had spoken to Nathan.

Matthew 1:1, 1:16 the book of the generation of Jesus Christ, **the son of David,** the son of Abraham. He was the son of promise. Jacob begat Joseph the husband of Mary of whom was born Jesus, who is called **Christ**.

Jesus came into the world and lived in it as a living example for God in holiness and righteousness that we to be endued with power from on high to live the Gospel in this world; God's way, fulfilling his purpose in all Godliness and righteousness.

We are in the world but was not of the world. We were created spiritual after God likeness; then the made body of flesh, the natural was applied to man. Man was made with the purpose of taking care of the earth.

Man in the image of God was told while being yet spirit beings both male and female to be fruitful and multiply and replenish the earth (**Gen. 1:27-28**). Jesus came to build God a spiritual house; that's why most of his work was done on the outside the organized Church. The world establish their own order that Jesus was sent to tear down.

There is a Church of the world and it's a loose Church. God's people like David started out reproducing after God's Order but have since; gone from under God's protection. Now their souls are in trouble. They have abused God's people that looked to them to hold up God's standard in the world.

God expects his people to be soul winners in his world. We are to be as Jesus was ready to tear down sin wherever it abound; whether in us or the world. Jesus went in the Temple and drove out them that sought gain in the Church.

THE BUILT UP SOUL

In this day living a godly holy life requires us to live as God ordained us to live. We are faced with so many deceptive means offered us by Satan; God's enemy. The battle for the soul of man continues even today. God has given us an ordained order in which man is to live.

Man today has changed the glory in f God into a lie and walked away from their God Ordained call and charge. Paul in **Romans 1:21** said because that when they knew God, they glorified Him not as God, neither were thankful but became vain in their imaginations and their foolish heart were darkened.

Man not only walked away from Holiness; but totally God! Sin separates God and man relationship through unholy living.

We can't say we love God and willfully sin. Sin is disobedience where we obey and do what we want rather than what God says we are to do. Simple disobedience is sin.

I have learned that I am in this world, but not of the world. I don't have to respond like man! I choose to do things God's way. Doing things his way makes me a winner and not the loser I was told I would be.

I have realized that this world is not my home. I have a knowledge of who God is and what he is to me. He is my rock: my all and all. This world is his and his alone!

THE BUILT UP SOUL

The World Belongs To God

Psalms 24:1 the earth is the Lord's and the fullness thereof and they that dwell therein. How do we can do what we want when it comes to God? Everything belong to our heavenly Father that created and made all thing.

The world consists of the universe, the heavens and all of mankind. It is the sphere of evil. We deal with evil on a daily basis; for men do it knowingly and unknowingly. When God created the world man was yet in his bosom..

Job 20:4-5 knowest thou not this pf old, that once man was placed upon earth that the triumphing of the wicked is short and the joy of the hypocrite but a moment. Why would we settle for less when God put all things in earth to Man's charge?

The way we think or desire things to be is not always the way of God. Folly is joy to him that is destitute of wisdom. He that loves pleasure in this world shall be a poor man. We must discern the company we keep. We must be ever so mindful of what's going on around us.

There are many things that increase vanity. Rejoice in our hearts, love God and people. Walk in the Will and Way of God in this world. The world rejoice and praises God too! Why do I say that? God is the God of man, beast, animal, the trees, everything in this world.

The earth purges with the rain, snow or whatever. The earth must be clean coming before God. How much more man? Man is also told to purge themselves of dead works.

Isaiah 32:9 he speaks even to the women to rise up from this at ease position they have taken. God wants women to hear his voice, give ear unto my speech. Everything in earth has purpose.

119

THE BUILT UP SOUL

This world is the Lord's and everything and everyone in earth. Be careful to do that which pleases God! We must take a closer look into our own doings and see if we died today would God be pleased?

There be many that have polluted the Gospel of Christ because of our own selfishness not to honor God. .

I Cor. 10:21-33 where injury to others is possible we must be careful to abstain even from things not wrong in themselves. What part of our senses have we allowed to be used by Satan today?

Have we spoken things or words out of our mouth that we should not have? Have we heard things today we shouldn't have heard? Have we looked upon things we should not have? Have we been sniffing around things we should not? Have we touched and handled things we ought not to have touched? Paul said in touch not, taste not, handle not.

Stop talking, being deceived and following men that is evil; evil communication corrupt good manners. *Jude 18-19* they told you there should be mockers in the last time, who should walk after their own ungodly lusts.

These be they who separate themselves, sensual, having not the Spirit. We don't have to go there, we choose to.

We are to abstain, refrain from some things, especially that which is evil or away from God. Abstaining from evil is an absolute necessity; for we know not the day or time our soul will be required of us.

THE BUILT UP SOUL

We must be ready at all times to answer heavens call.

Love like God love that we be not caught up in the Devil's web of lies, deceit, and murder. He sets out against us each day to make us give up the Holy Ghost. He wants our soul!

When we practice ungodliness in the flesh, and sin against God, we open up the gate for Satan to use our senses.

We are to put a difference between clean and unclean, holy and unholy in this world that we get to go into God's world in heaven..

We as Christians must always put God first in our lives. Do as He say we are to do. Answer every man with the wisdom of God, thereby abstaining from our own thinking and doing.

Christian liberty is not lessened by such voluntary abstinence for the good of others. On the other side though don't be pulled into their things either that will cause us to sin.

We are to regard God and our fellow man in our acts and doings. Our purpose is to do the Will of God always.

We do all things for God's glory! God called or chose us to be soul winners, pleasing God! We are to seek God out of our soul!

Let's do an inventory of our life today!

THE BUILT UP SOUL

How's Our Living

In this day living a godly holy life requires us to live as God ordained us to live. We are faced with so many deceptive means offered us by Satan; God's enemy. The battle for the soul of man continues even today. God has given us an ordained order in which man is to live.

Man today has changed the glory of God into a lie and walked away from their God Ordained call and charge.

Paul in **Romans 1:21 said because that when they knew God, they glorified Him not as God, neither were thankful but became vain in their imaginations and their foolish heart were darkened.**

Man not only walked away from Holiness; but totally God! Sin separates God and man relationship through unholy living.

We can't say we love God and willfully sin. Sin is disobedience where we don't obey and on the contrary do what we want rather than what God says we are to do.

Simple disobedience is sin. When God told Ananias (**Acts 9:10-17**) to go to one called Saul; he was afraid. Spiritual assignments ignored is sin right own even when only you and God knows.

How times come back again that we which didn't pass the test the first time have a chance to get it right. There is nothing new under the heavens. If God has set us free; are not we free indeed? Why then do we seek to be bound? Sin bind us up and sin will keep us bound!

Even in our speech we bind our self up and blame everybody of our own doings. God requires holiness in the life of every man (male) and woman (female)! If I want to be perfect in life I must perfect my life to be as God said and not as man says I can have it.

THE BUILT UP SOUL

He require parents to train up the children to love, honor, reverence and obey Him early in life that they forget Him not.

God wants to be first in the heart of mankind; as Creator and Lord He should be. God loves us all, no matter what we appear to be outwardly. God wants to be glorified as He created man to do.

Everything that takes us away from glorifying God in Spirit and in Truth is sin; which glorify Satan instead. An unholy lifestyle prepare us for he'll!

Satan, and all the disobedient angels has been adjudged for hell. Satan plan to enlarge his little territory with the souls of disobedient man. We then have to work against Satan that seek us to disobey God. He knows of the perfect disobedience that will keep man out of heaven; after all he was kicked out!

Holiness is a lifestyle ruled and governed by God through His Holy Word and Holy Spirit that we must submit authority to in the earth now that we live to live again with God in heaven.

God created us to the praise of His glory spiritually; then made a body man was to maneuver with in earth. God then breathed His Spirit in man and man became a living soul; holy unto God! Holiness was the only lifestyle man knew until they disobeyed God.

Man knew not what they did until a change happen to them after Adam had eaten of the forbidden fruit. We now know better because Jesus the second Adam had come! Holiness is right; do better! Live!

THE BUILT UP SOUL

Holiness God's Ordained Way

Yes! God has a way! That way is a call to all men alike. God said we are to be as He is; Holy in all areas of life, in every state of being totally; mind, body, heart, soul and spirit. Do we even realize we are five parts in one?

God created man a spirit being in his image, He gave us a mind after himself; for it was to guide man, He gave us a heart after him to love him, He made us a body to please Him in our flesh and take care the earth he framed up; providing us a home and He gave man a soul that would one day be with him for eternity.

Man is someone dear and special to God. Man was put here in earth to rule the earth by way of Holiness unto the Lord God. Adam himself knew he was a man and God was his Creator for he spent time with God in the cool of the day every evening.

God saw his loneliness (*Gen. 2:*18) and took from his body that other created part He had inserted within Adam after He made him a body called a rib (*Gen. 2:21*).

He designed another body unlike the first and put the rib taken from Adam inside that body (*Gen. 2:22*). He took that body and lay beside Adam and Adam called her woman because she was a living womb for reproduction (*Gen. 2:23-24*).

She became his wife (*Gen. 2:24*). She is now on the outside of him. The once one male/female is now two, man and woman. There is no confusion in God nor division in the Spirit of the two flesh beings. They are one Spirit that was made two in flesh.

In Spirit man is in obedience already to God. Now he is being taught obedience to God in the flesh. We have a two-fold requirement in life. We must obey God spiritually and naturally to fulfill his Holiness in the earth.

THE BUILT UP SOUL

Without both now being in submission to God we cannot please God as Adam himself found out.

Just as He had birth forth woman, they were to birth forth Holiness everyday. They were so Holy and dead to the flesh they didn't know of their nakedness (*Gen. 2:25*). They were alive spiritually but knew not the naturally flesh nature.

One day they took a walk that changed their lives forever. They met a stranger that talked to Eve while he (Adam) stood by listening (*Gen. 3:1-6*). He brought no correction to her. She was allowed to continue her conversation with the serpent (aka called snake now).

Adam nor Eve knew of Satan, for they had only been told by God to obey what He said; concerning the tree in the midst of the Garden (*Gen. 2:16-17*); the tree of the knowledge of good and evil. He told Adam not to eat of it; for in the day that thou eat of it, you shall surely die. Eve was still on the inside of Adam spiritually so she knew too!

Many have asked how did she know? She repeated what God has said to the serpent (*Gen. 3:2-3*). No man have seen God at anytime but spiritually we hear Him speak. We believe it's Him. Eve had heard what God said to Adam; they were one spiritually. Understand God can talk to us separately apart and we come together in one accord and speak the same thing hours and miles apart at the same time.

Now Satan with his convincing conniving lying pronounced self had gotten her to speak. He being more subtle than they knew God and understood that He meant they would die a spiritual death as He had done.

Many say why did God allow Satan to be free and the other Angels be chained up? Satan has brought them a lie but they were without excuse for in heaven they knew better.

Even now with Adam it was a test of obedience and allegiance to God. Adam and Eve knew the spiritual not natural flesh. That's why they would die if they disobeyed.

Even though Eve ate first; nothing happened as God had said would happen. Eve was inside, heard the Word spoken but God was speaking to Adam as the head of the woman.

He was charged to keep her in line. Satan had discovered early that He knew not of godly Order.

He looked and knew they knew not they were naked. He heard too what God had spoken to them. He heard too what God had not told them because he knew God better than any man.

He also knew what it meant to be in obedience. He knew of God's wrath first hand.

The knowledge he had of God and the understanding of that knowledge gave him the ups on the first man as well as now. How dare he, God put man over him! How do we know this? Jesus came and Jesus died to put Satan back under our feet (*Rom. 16:20*).

Now we see his work of deception against man and understand why he do what he do to keep man from living a pure godly, holy lifestyle of Holiness. He has deceived man from the beginning starting with Adam.

He used that which came out of man to deceive him into going against what God had said he was to obey.

The woman had been Adam's all and all in the earth. He was happy. That's why women are so hard pressed and found out by man yet today. If she say she is Holy and sanctified a man will test that relationship.

The test is one of truth and faithfulness. Adam was deceived by what he didn't see! He saw nothing happen to Eve; she didn't die.

Surely God has said in the day ye eat thereof he shall surely die (**Gen. 2:17**). Satan used what God has said to paint God to man as a liar and a deceiver that He would steal our faith and trust away from God.

He wants man soul and he uses our bodies against us to make us disobey what God has said.

Adam eyes; he was deceived by his sense of sight. Now the eyes of both Adam and Eve were opened and they knew that they were naked for the first time naturally. As well they were stripped of their pure Holy relationship in the Spirit with God. They had been blind to life as they knew it; stress free in the Spirit.

They lost their covering of joy, peace and righteousness in the Holy Ghost for the whole of mankind! But thanks be unto God who had a plan of redemption to come for man that would come to Him (Christ) and obey God the Father again!

Because one man Adam disobeyed it set in order the sin and same judgment to man Satan had. When are we going to awake out of sleep? Adam and Eve had God but was ignorant of Satan and his devices.

Had they just trusted God at his Word everything would have been alright. But now they reaped dear punishment for their acts of disobedience.

When time came for them to meet God in his assigned place where he brought his wife with him; they hid from God instead (**Gen. 3:9-11**). God had his own ordained way man was to take. He didn't tell them they were naked; so how did they know?

God knew what they had done but they had to confess it before Him at his throne. They died a spiritual death; the Spirit had departed. They couldn't feel Him deep within on the inside as they had before they ate of the tree. Sin separates man still today from God.

Now sin when it is conceived brings forth death still today. It not only killed Adam's awesome spiritual life but man's still today! Adam was punished as well as Eve and the serpent. His list as we will note was longer and more severe than theirs.

The serpent (**Gen. 3:14**) the Lord said would no longer stand upright but crawl on its belly being the most cursed animal found eating dust all the days of their life. Every serpent now called snake suffered God's wrath because of one being used by Satan.

Eve would face sorrow (**Gen. 3:16**) he said would come in childbirth. Unto the woman I will greatly multiply that sorrow and that conception. The woman's desire shall be to her husband and he shall rule over them.

God put enmity (**Gen. 3:15**), the bitter attitude or feelings of an enemy or of mutual enemies, hostility or antagonism; between thee and the woman, and between thy seed and her seed; it shall bruise thy head and thou shall bruise his head.

Adam was cursed thirdly and last (**Gen. 3:19-19**); he would not eat off the tree of life, he was cursed with death he would never have known, eat of sorrow all the days of life, man would have thorns and thistles brought forth d the tree and he would eat of the herbs of the field. He would work until he died. He would return to the dust he was made of.

THE BUILT UP SOUL

There is today still a lot today enmity, hostility, animosity, and antagonism existing from the curse put on mankind. Satan uses these things to keep man and woman separate and apart outside of Holiness.

There is strong settled feelings of hatred among man today with the differences we can see of the seed come through the bloodline of the first man and woman.

Whether it is concealed, displayed, or latent; it's there. Hostility expressed in active opposition is present today in the form of racial attacks.

There is much bitterness active and real in the world today. There is so much animosity tending to break out in open hostility. The real antagonistic force behind what happen in the Garden of Eden and now is Satan.

He still stand behind the scene trying to steal the soul of man by way of deception through His own hate for us. He have mutual dislike of all men. God though has a way to bring us out.

Have not we been deceived long enough? Just as Adam heartened to the voice of His wife, man still today listen to the voice of the enemy; one called Satan and continue in disobedience to what God has commanded us to not do.

Thou shall not do as Adam and Eve did by putting something before God. Don't except the lie of Satan; rather believe the truth of God. Don't take the path Satan lead and desire us to take; it will surely take us away from God and Holiness.

Don't bow down to the pleasure of Satan; nor serve him or his masteries.

Don't lie, steal or deceive yourself or another. Keep our life holy, sanctified; living everyday as if it's our last day upon the earth. Hear man, but hear God more that we

129

THE BUILT UP SOUL

know the truth that will make us free, setting us free from sin that promises us a home in he'll eternally for the same disobedience Satan faced.

Just as the serpent, Adam and Eve had to confess their wrongful deeds before God; so must we. Stay free with God on our side. To be free we must express sorrow in our wrong doings, repent them and quit them.

It's bad enough we will suffer from the sin we have done in life while we live; but do we really think we want the suffer for them after we die?

Repent it and quit it while the blood is running in our veins. Choose Holiness!

THE BUILT UP SOUL

Holiness; A Way Of Life

No man knows the day or hour the Son of man will return to earth. There is a way He expect us to be found when He come calling! Holiness calls us to a place of purity, cleanness, chastity and right living. Holiness consist of righteousness, sanctification and justification. God requires that as He is Holy that we be too!

Isaiah 35:8 and an highway shall be there and a way and it shall be called The Way of Holiness; the unclean shall not pass over it, but it shall be for those; the wayfaring men, though fools, shall not eat therein!

Isaiah was king among the Prophets and Israel celebrated him more than any other of them. This book that is named after him is the profoundest of all Hebrew literature. It teaches one theme; salvation by faith throughout the book. He carried the vision of God

He had access to the King of Israel and had close intimacy with the Priests (*Isa. 7:3; 8:2*). He received his call to the prophetic office in a Temple service which he accepted with a praiseworthy alacrity; accepting his commission without any hesitation. He knew that his task would be one of fruitless warnings and exhortation.

If we think we can sin and blame it on ignorance; think again! Man is without excuse for willfully, knowingly disobeying God's Word. We are held accountable to know after God sent his Son to redeem us.

Isaiah 34:1-2 tell us we have to come and hearken all, every one therein that lives all over the world to the voice of the Lord. His indignation is upon all nations and his fury upon all their armies, God will utterly destroy the enemies of his Word and deliver them to the slaughter which we know to be hell.

In the world today both Christian and non-Christian is being card back to the Way of Holiness. We can't crossover outside the threshold of God; that is being in compliance to his Word. Holiness is a way of life set by our Creator; God Himself.

He is our Counselor and Strength. Come to Him wholehearted and He will give us strength for the battle. He will preserve our souls. He is our shield and help in the time of trouble. He will strengthen our hands.

Be strong and fear not Isaiah said to the fearful and weak among them (*Isa. 35:1-7*), the eyes of the blind shall be opened and the ears of the deaf unstopped, the lame man shall leap, and the tongue of the dumb shall sing. We need to find that right path no matter our deficiency and God will fix us and keep us in the Way Of Holiness his way!

Why would Isaiah have to encourage God's own people in the Way of Holiness? Surely if God is Holy, his people are! But that's not always the case. God has a standard his people must continuously hold fast to. His people forsook the Way and followed after the world.

God gave Isaiah a vision of His people that had left their first love; Him. *Isaiah 1:2* hear, O heaven and give ear, O earth: for the Lord hath spoken, I have nourished and brought up children and they have rebelled against me. God said animals know their owners, but my people don't know me nor consider me.

How can we have a father and not know him? Many don't today naturally know who their father are either. Many that name the Name of Christ don't really know Him or desire to know Him in the fullness thereof. They don't want to know Him inwardly because aren't willing or ready to fully commit to the Way of Holiness in the strictness of its call.

Just as the people of Israel was here in the book of Isaiah man resist God's Way of Holiness today. *Isaiah*

THE BUILT UP SOUL

1:4-5 ah sinful nation, a people laden with iniquity. A seed of evildoers, children that are corrupters; they have forsaken the Lord, they have provoked the Holy One of Israel unto anger, they are gone away backward. Is this happening right now in your nation? It is mine!

God is calling man back to that first created state of Holiness when they knew no sin. Man today lack soundness from the sole of their feet to the head. We really are suppose to think and know where to lead our feet; not the other way around. From the old to the very young we lack continuity in knowing the distinctive characteristics of God and His Way of Holiness.

We don't make the noise of a Saint of God required of a Christian. God's noise is an identifiable one of praise, worship, glorification and right living Hid Holy ordained Way outlined in his Holy Word. All of our worship should be done in the Spirit. The praise should be Spirit led, Spirit controlled, and Spirit filled. It's a way that seem right to man but the end thereof is the way of death. The noise made to God has a reflex that carry one back to the world. Watch that demon!

God wants to live in our heart where obedience keep us within earshot of hearing Him. We must live where the Spirit continue to dwell in us leading and guiding our every move. It's the walk of Holiness God's Way. God wants man free from defect, free from sin, free that we can obtain and keep his God given grace; not abuse it.

We are to be as two wide channels linked together as one straight body and sin free because the mainland of sin has been destroyed by The long inlet and arm of Jesus Christ that was hung high and stretched wide. He covered every area of sin to give man the soundness to reject sin.

Have we ever wondered why we don't have to teach a baby to say "no"? Saying no is what God required of man since the beginning; all Eve had to say was "no" to the serpent. All Adam had to do is say "no" to Eve and there would never have been no sin. There would be no need for us to learn to say "no" to sin. No is the response we need caught up in our vocabulary to maintain our state of Holiness!

It's time we become spiritually sound in our relationship with God; it is a requirement for heaven. Isaiah getting close to closing out his book reminds us not to be derelict in our duty to God. God's ears is open to our call; we can return to him and do it right. God has power to deliver; He is waiting on us. Isaiah still today proclaims the coming Christ and exhort us to trust in God; not human resources for God can dry them up. Believe that!

Its time to awake out of sleep; put on the arm of the Lord for his redeemed has come and shall return again. *Isaiah 51:12* I, even I am he that comforteth you: who art thou, that thou shouldest be afraid of a man that shall die, and the son of man which shall be made as grass?

We better believe and trust God! Man will cause us to forget God! Awake out of the drunken stupor of sin today. Why live in sin, be unhappy, die in sin and spend eternity in hell? Christ died defending man; accept the free redemption he has given to everyone that will receive.

This is what the Way of Holiness is about. If we shake ourselves free of the dust that surrounds the truth of who we are, we can allow God to reign over our life in true Holiness. Even leaders will know and recognize the rue and living God in this time of life. The prophecy Isaiah (*Isa. 52:13*-15) gave is a prophecy of Christ glory that all would come to know as true. *Luke 22:19* Jesus himself reminds us of what Isaiah prophesied when he told the Disciples "this is my body which is broken for you: this do in remembrance of me".

THE BUILT UP SOUL

Jesus offered Holiness as a Way of life again to all that
would accept him, believe on him. Confess him before
men and deny themselves of their own way. He would
be wounded for our transgressions as spoken forth by
God out of the mouth of Isaiah (*Isa. 53:5*) and He was
indeed. But it carry a further message; he was bruised
for our iniquities, the chastisement of our peace was
upon him and with his stripes we are healed; all sin and
sickness!

It pleased God to allow this to come about for our sake
that the enemy of our soul be laid to rest in our life. How
much more should we do to please Him in our living?
God guarantee us victory where he will uncorrupt our
eyesight where we have a forgiving unforgotten moment.

God requires we live in righteousness; he brought
righteousness to us. God requires Holiness as a Way of
life for man; He sent Jesus as the Way lived as a living
sacrifice in flesh to show us the Way.

God requires us to deny our self fleshly wants; He
showed us repentance of our way through Jesus that
repented for asking for the cup of death be passed over.
God doesn't ask man to do anything He himself hasn't
done. He is giving us a call to faith and repentance!
Jesus is our intercessor.

Isaiah 55:6-9 Seek ye tbe Lord while he may be found,
call ye upon him while he is near; let the wicked forsake
his way and the unrighteous man his thoughts and let
him return unto the Lord; and he will have mercy upon
him and to our God; for he will abundantly pardon. For
my thoughts are not your thoughts; neither are your
ways said the Lord. For as the heavens are higher than
the earth, so are my ways higher than your ways and my
thoughts than your thoughts.

THE BUILT UP SOUL

Jesus Took A Second Look

Matthew 26:30b O my Father, if it be possible let this cup pass from me; nevertheless not as I will, but as thou will.

As a leader your life is always under the spotlight. Although they have a multitask existence with family and friends; leaders yet have an accountability to God to do that which God requires as God requires them.

Rather its favorable with man or not, it still must be done.

Let's look at Jesus! Jesus lived his life in order to the Word He was but toward the end of his of his earthly journey he actually desired to do things his way in his desire to stay in the earth with his Disciples. He knew they weren't ready to take on the world. His flesh desired to remain.

Matthew 26:36-47 Jesus had gone to that place called Gethsemane. He told his Disciples to sit here while He went to go pray. We need alone time with God in prayer and study. He took Peter and two others with him. He told them my soul is exceedingly sorrowful. He told them to stay; tarry here and watch with me.

We must be careful of the people we take into our bosom to follow us. They must be in one accord with us. He came to a place away from them and fell on his knees and prayed to God; His Father. O my Father, if it be possible let this cup pass from me; nevertheless not as I will, but as thou will.

This was a cry in the flesh although he was come from God directly. This is what Adam dealt with also. He came back to the Disciples and they were asleep. He said "what could not you watch with me one hour"?

THE BUILT UP SOUL

Watch and pray Jesus said that we enter not into temptation; the SPIRIT indeed is willing, but the flesh is weak. He went away to pray again. Repenting he said, "O my Father, if this cup may not pass away from me except I drink it, thy Will be done"! Sometime we need to take a second look and re-access ourselves to make sure we are within God's Will.

He came and found them yet sleeping a third time. They were so sleepy! How many times do we find ourselves sleeping through the revolution rather than open-eyed and praying for change in the situation?

It's like that today in the time we live. God's people is asleep on the job of soul winning!

We have been called to win souls for Christ. We are to work while it is day! Jesus told his Disciples to sleep on, take your rest; at that time He was their watch. Behold the hour was upon them when He, the Son of man is betrayed as He had told them a few passages before.

Now he was telling them that the time had come. Rise, let us be going; behold he is at hand that does betray me! When God calls we have to listen carefully that we fall into obedience where God will be glorified.

In this time, as in the day of Jesus we need to take a new look at things. Jesus, the second Adam came into the world birth of the Spirit as Adam was to restore that once lost relationship between God and man.

His life too was quiet until he began to do what he was sent to do.

Notice all of the uproar that surrounds our new President, Donald Trump. People labeled Jesus as the carpenter Joseph son. Yet he was not his son but one sent of God for a specific work. In this time God is yet calling man to obedience and accountability.

God can use what He want, when He want, how he want, who He want and where He wants to use them. He uses man but he can use a mule, donkey, or stone for He is God.

Satan broke the glorification between God and Man. God used his only begotten Son sent to redeem man back to right relationship with Him. Here Satan yet again tried keeping us separated with the split of disobedience.

He has in the beginning, even then with Jesus and us today worked hard to shred any hope of eternal life with God for man. How long will we allow him to keep us bound where we can't see God as we should?

Its not God that sleep; but man! Man is just like us; flesh. But Jesus took a second look at flesh and remembered who He was and his purpose. Man today need to take that second look at Christ too; that we see God as He is; Reverent!

We look and see Adam that brought flesh alive (**Gen. 3:8-12**) in us and now need to see Jesus the second Adam after the Spirit that came to bring flesh back under subjection to God with the help of the Holy Spirit that made man alive; living souls!

Jesus realized that man is weak because of the flesh. They are earthly as the dust and water their bodies were made of. He gave them one simple task; pray with me. They in their weakened body had to rest so they fell asleep when they needed to be doing as He requested.

Many God ordained Change Agents, the called and chosen of God are sleep concerning the things of God.

THE BUILT UP SOUL

Many have gone from under the protection of God as they seek man's ok for what they do in the Name of Jesus. This Jesus dealt with then as now. He was crucified for calling men back into right relationship to the Father, God!

In his journey he loved walking among mankind and giving them the Way. He loved bringing them out of the darkness of sin to righteousness in the light of God. He loved bringing them the Truth, which Satan tried to make a lie.

This passage is also symbolic of Christ return to earth again. How will He find us? Will we too be asleep when we should be about God's business?

Matthew 3:15 Jesus talking to John when He was to be Baptized said suffer it to be so now, for thus it becometh us to fulfill all righteousness.

John didn't feel worthy enough to Baptize Jesus. Jesus submitted to Baptism permitting man to see his inward conviction whereas his Father was concerned.

God made the announcement to the world though the Holy Spirit of God descending (coming down from heaven) like a visible dove and lighting upon Him. A voice from Heaven declared that this is my beloved Son in whom I am well pleased. What will He have to say about us?

Jesus said we are the salt of the earth (**Matt. 5:13**) but if the salt has lost its flavor where with shall it be salted? It is thenceforth good for nothing, but to be cast out, and to be trodden under the foot of men.

Holiness is rightly a Way of life. We are seasoned in righteousness and God's promise of eternal life is sure.

THE BUILT UP SOUL

When we walk in righteousness it mean we have taken a second look at our life being lived after the Order of God according to His Holy Word.

Right living keeps us salted for Heaven. It causes us to live peace with one another. We are fueled by the fire of the Holy Ghost that will lead and guide us to Heaven.

Take a second look at salvation and see if we are in compliance today. We should have a desire like Jesus did to fulfill God's purpose rather than that of man. We should thirst after that which ultimately please God no matter how distasteful it is in the flesh.

Realize that the second look Jesus took made us free where we are free indeed from the bondage sin presents. God sanctified Jesus and sent him into the world (*John 10:36*) that we too can choose to be sanctified; set apart from the world. As in the beginning we are in the world but not of the world.

Adam was in the world but knew not that he was a man made of flesh; for he was a created spirit being (*Gen. 3:22*). God said behold man has become as one of us, to know good and evil that God had covered them from knowing flesh where it would be served more than Spirit in God's presence.

Adam lost his place in that blessed place forever for mankind; but God! God took a second look at man and gave us that choice again to choose Him. He call for obedience from man.

When we look and see as God sees we will deny our self, pick up the Cross and follow Jesus, the second Adam that have cleansed us through the Word!

When we take a second look at Jesus we see God in a more significant way where we abide in Him and He in us. We must take a second look and realize as Jesus

140

did that we can do nothing in and of our self. We need God! We have been sanctified through the Truth of Christ, accepted, believed on and confessed.

As Jesus was sent into the world that we be saved; He sends us out too to offer that same salvation to lost men everywhere. He don't want us asleep, sleeping through the revolution of sin! Teach others that they are to worship God. We are to seek Him as Jesus did and not look for men strength to carry us through life. We are to look unto God; the Author and finisher of our faith.

Jesus encourages us in (**Matt. 6:33**) to seek ye first the Kingdom of God and His righteousness and all these things shall be added unto you. Whosoever he said that will come after me have denied themselves. They have taken a second look as Jesus did. What He saw gave him strength to go forward; we too can go forward in Christ.

Whosoever will lose their life for the Gospel sake will save their soul. For whosoever believe that God sent his only begotten Son because He loved man so much; shall not perish but have everlasting life. Jesus didn't come to condemn man, but through him tbey might be saved.

Jesus is the Way, the Truth, and the Light and this is the way he found those that walked with Him; asleep! Will we too sleep? This is the condemnation that light has come into the world but men love darkness rather than light, because their deeds were evil which is represented as sleep. Adam slept, but Jesus the second Adam was awake. He brought back to man the way of perfection; perfection in the Word by way of the Holy Spirit the continuator of the work of God and Christ.

THE BUILT UP SOUL

Where Is The Sense

Matthew 7:22-23 many will say to me in that day, Lord, Lord, have we not prophesied in thy Name? And in thy Name has cast out devils? And in thy Name done many wonderful works? And then will I profess unto them, I never knew you; depart from me, ye that work iniquity.

How we see God is not represented in man's senses. The seeing eye is not subtle enough (SENSE). We cannot rely or depend on our senses for heavenly manner.

God is not served by what we see, feel, touch, handle, hear, or comprehend in our natural mind. We must take heed and beware of what we presume to be God.

We have not seen God physically. We can't screen him emotionally or psychologically. We can only have him spiritually. We accept Him as He is, we believe that He is, and we confess Him as the Lord that He is.

How do we do that? We take Him at His Word, deny us our wants and desires for what He want. Do as God says, not as man says. Seek God's Word for answers.

We except what His Word says as truth. We make His Word the Gospel! We have Holiness as our way of life. We are not ignorant of Satan's devices.

We don't justify sin for **Proverbs 17:**15 says he that justifieth the wicked, and he that condemneth the just, even they both are abomination to the Lord! We cannot accept sin, no matter who does

142

THE BUILT UP SOUL

it. Being agreeable to sin pulls us into that sin as if we our self committed the act. Let's be careful to glorify God in our natural bodies.

Now doing things God's way; we are happy in the Lord each and every day! We must be careful not to side with man in that which goes against God. That's seeing things Satan's way. Sin is still sin everyday no matter who does it.

The seer sees as God sees; not to change the purpose but to fulfill it according to God's Will. How do we know God's Will? We take His Word and study to know it concerning our lives and change what need to be changed.

His Will is contained in His Word completely. We cannot use our senses to be a servant of God.

We must deny self! Self stands in God's way. Self guided by our senses keep us from seeking the Word; so it blocks the Spirit that keeps us alive in Christ. Except we exceed our self we can't see God.

Man have there own righteousness that goes against the Order of God. Man make laws that goes against God and think they're right.

Man has their own righteousness. If the right thing come to them, they reject it unless it comes from one they hold high regard for. The unacceptable is acceptable if its their friend or loved one.

When we follow our own senses Holiness is not the way we take, for in our senses Holiness is foolishness to man. We have to escape our senses to see as God sees in the Spirit.

Everything that appears beautiful outwardly is not real.

Matthew 23:27-28 woe unto you scribes and Pharisees, hypocrites, for ye are likened unto white sepulchres, which indeed appear beautiful outward, but are within full of dead men's bones, and of all uncleanness.

Even so ye also outwardly appear righteous unto men, but within ye are full of hypocrisy and iniquity.

Our senses keep us from appearing Godly as God requires. Man is to see God in and through us.

Man can be fooled but God is not. This action keeps us out of heaven! We are to seek the abundance of God in our offering. We are our own witness of who Christ is in our life.

Luke 16:15 ye are they which justify yourselves before men: but God knows your hearts; for that which is highly esteemed among men is abomination in the sight of God. Man pray to God out of their senses within themselves. Its about I, me instead of us, we.

Jesus said in *John 6:38* for I came down from heaven, not to do mine own Will, but the will of him that sent me. If Jesus had to come from under his own senses what about us?

THE BUILT UP SOUL

We are warned not to lay up for ourselves treasures in the earth. We are told to lay up for ourselves treasure in heaven that no one can steal (**Matt. 6:19**). For where our treasure is, there will our heart be also.

Many profess that the work they do for Christ is for Him, but it is secretly of their own desire. You will know the work by the sacrifices made. If we be in doubt concerning anything we are told to go to the Lord (**Luke 12:29-32**).

It is God's good pleasure to give us all we can ask or think. The world love its own and seek after that which will prosper them; not God.

Like a product that await hitting the shelf in the world, every aspect of God must be known that man will believe.

How can we really reject God if we know Him? We do! If we drop our senses and surrender our heart, soul, mind, body and spirit to God, we take on his mind that will regulate every part of us by calling us in obedience to his Word.

Jesus in his time of temptation where Satan wanted him to work before time, spoke back (**Matthew 4:4**) to Satan the tempter after he told him if thou be the Son of God, (he knew who Jesus was) command that these stones be made bread.

Jesus answered and said "it is written, man shall not live by bread alone, but by every Word that proceeded out of the mouth of God. Senses is for God's use!

When are we going to realize that our life is not about us; its all about God? It is he that gave his Spirit that we be alive; a living stone! It is in Him we live, move and have our being.

When are we going to realize that Satan means us no good? When are we going to realize our battles in life is to tear down God's Kingdom, not build one for us? He hates us.

God is not man's enemy; Satan is. He comes to lie on God, steal man's relationship with God and rob us of who God really is.

He deceive man to make us curse God and die. Realize God created and made man to take Satan's place in glorifying Him.

THE BUILT UP SOUL

The World Was Before Man

God didn't create anything after man. Man was last and very much different than the animals or trees. When man want to do things outside of what God has said they will offer some strange stuff and say it is God to do what they want to do.

Genesis 1:2-9 and the earth was without form, and void; and darkness was upon the face of the deep, and the Spirit of the Lord moved upon the face of the waters, so the waters was here before man.

God said let there be light and there was light. He divided the light from the darkness calling light; day and darkness; night. The evening and the morning was the first day.

God continued his work saying, let there be a firmament in the midst of the waters and let it divide the waters from the waters. The divided waters were either under the firmament or above it. God called the firmament Heaven.

He then called for the waters under the Heavens to be gathered together in one place, that the dry land appear, and it was so.

Isaiah 40:13-14 asks a question; who hath directed the Spirit of the Lord? Or being his counsellor hath taught him? With whom took He counsel, and who instructed Him, and taught Him in the path of judgment? Who has taught God knowledge? Who is it that have showed God the way of understanding?

David in **Psalm 33:6-9** makes us know that all things were made by the Word of Lord and all the hosts pf them by the breath of his mouth. He tells us that we should stand in awe of God for it was He that spoke and it was done; he commanded and things got done.

Paul in **Hebrews 11:3** said through faith we understand that the worlds were framed by the Word of God, so that things which are seen were not made of things which do appear.

Everything on earth gives obeisance to God at their appointed time except man.

The sun rises and sets on time as God desires it to. The moon comes up and goes in as God desires it to. It rains when God says so, where and how he says. The earth quakes as God orders it. What is wrong with man? Man have need to obey also!

Remember Cain and Abel brought God as Lord; a sacrifice of their first fruit to show his love and appreciation referencing him as Lord. We too must offer him a sacrifice of love; through right living.

God gave the sea a decree, that the waters shouldn't pass his Commandments, when he appointed the foundations of the earth; (**Prov. 8: 29**). How much more do He require of us? Just as everything obey God we too must obey.

God expect us to give Him not only our best offering; He wants Himself to be our all and all.

THE BUILT UP SOUL

Man's Shortcomings

Genesis 3:4-6

Eve desiring to eat of the forbidden fruit caught the attention of Satan. We have all suffered the consequences of her desire. We have all suffered the defrauding act of Jacob in his deception of stealing the blessing of his father from Esau.

We covet man's position in the earth, but one I am sure no one else wants is Judas' when he betrayed Jesus for thirty pieces of silver. We desire spots and position that will forever affect our lives and others whether it is good or bad. We choose and we are responsible for our acts.

Evil upon the people is a promise from God to all that reject Him and disobey his Law. **Leviticus 26:37** we shall have no power to stand before our enemies.

When our hearts is not convicted toward God we will do anything we want to; right or wrong and think nothing of it. Because of this we allow evil (that which is morally wrong or bad, wicked and depraved) to enter into our hearts. We will cause harm or pain to another and think nothing of it.

How much more our acts allow Satan access to cause injurious trouble that may be offensive or disgusting to come our way. Whereas God would have prevented this evil foe from triumphing over us, he folds his hands. What have we done?

We develop the evil that finds itself coming our way for we don't abstain from it. Our unfruitful thoughts where we think we will not walk in the way of good men and keep the path of the righteous takes us down a road from good to evil. We have a choice to choose good over evil and it starts in our thinking.

THE BUILT UP SOUL

When God say love your enemies he means just that. Our thoughts carry us off track; love who I want to and crucify the rest. He also said do good to them that hate you as He does for us that have rejected Him. He reign over the just and unjust; raining down from heaven to meet the need of them as he has from the beginning.

Luke 6:27-29 but I say unto you which hear, love your enemies, do good to them which hate you, bless them that curse you, and pray for them which despitefully use you. And unto him that smite thee on the one cheek, offer also the other and him that taketh away thy cloak; forbid him not to take thy coat also.

THE BUILT UP SOUL

Man, Lost In The World

Life and death both is a mystery to man because no one can pinpoint the day and hour they will be born or the day they die. We can't say how long we will live after we are born. We have a promise of seventy years now but we once were to live one hundred twenty years.

Another thing is we don't know how we will go; some people die of old, some of sickness to the body, some murdered, some at birth, or for other reasons associated with the flesh. Do we really die?

We would never have thought some years ago that we as parents would outlive our children; never given it a thought. Only God knows the day and hour of our departure. Only God knows when we will be born. Only God knows how we will leave earth.

Only God knows the pain felt after a loved one has left us. Why do we have pain? We have pain in our heart because in actuality a part of our heart is gone away; yet that part is still there. We have pain because they have been with us in the flesh.

Every part of their life shared with us is a visible part of our life. We could touch them, hug them, laugh with them, hear their words when they speak, and we can hear the patter of their feet walking towards us or running away from us. They are a living part of our lives.

We miss them although they are still a vital part of us. Gone in body but very much alive in spirit. Who know the day or hour we too will depart this earth in body? We are in the world but not of the world so we depart to go to a spiritual world. The body for earth and the soul for heaven.

In life we love all those we come in contact with. We are lost in the world without God and people. In life we leave a legacy, a memory, and a joy to have known one another. In death we take so much away from those we love, but we leave our love that will carry on a lifetime after we are gone. For all that knew us remember a part of what we have done in this life.

What we will be remembered for in the hearts and minds of people is predicated upon how we live our life. Most people eventually will remember the good we have done as opposed to the bad we have done. The good usually outweigh the bad somewhere down the line.

Most people sing a song "may the good I've done speak for me". Well with God; good is not good enough. There is usually more we can do with what we have been given to work with. When we fail to work that which pleases God we are lost in the world. Our purpose is muted.

No we don't know the day or the hour we will come into the world or the time we will leave but what matters with God is the in between; the quality of life lived for Him.

For what profit is there if we gain the whole world and lose our own soul, Matthew 16:26? We as a people worry about the wrong things. We worry about what we have here in the

THE BUILT UP SOUL

earth materially, financially, physically, emotionally, or psychologically. What we don't give consideration to is our spiritual makeup. As we live our love ones are a part of our heart. They live there, they dwell there. That's just how God wants to dwell in our hearts.

He wants us to love him so much more than how we love those that are with us today and gone tomorrow. He wants to be a vital part of our makeup too!

We don't know the day or hour for our arrival or departure but one thing for sure; Christ had better be a part of our living and dying. Christ being a vital part of our lives makes a difference in our dying.

Having things is nothing compared to having Christ that brings forth the Kingdom of Heaven to us. The Kingdom of Heaven is love, joy, peace and righteousness in the Holy Ghost.

We can't find no greater love than the Love of God. There is no greater joy than the Joy of the Lord. There is no greater peace; for He is our Peace. There is none righteous but God, so He is our Righteousness.

Christ in us is the hope of Glory. Jesus dying is our Salvation and Redemption. He is our charger for the battery of our heart. He charges us to keep his Word, do His Commandments, and follow on to know Him.

He doesn't ask anything too hard of us; for to do the things is not hard when our hearts are fixed towards Him. We don't know the day or the time we

153

will depart this world as we know it but we can be ready to go! Will you be ready? The call will be made and the trumpet will sound; will you heed? I say to you today, be ready and willing to take the next step of life, it's the best part.

Come to Jesus today, accept Christ as Lord, believe on Him, and confess your sin and be healed, delivered, and set free. Be sure that when the day and hour come you will be ready! We must make up our minds that nobody is worth my soul in hell. We are living in the tenth hour of the day and tomorrow are not promised.

Everyday known to man as we know it is tomorrow and tomorrow always come as today. So when is tomorrow really? You see yesterday we found out that death has no sorrow that heaven cannot heal. We look at death as a sorrowful thing, but why when it took a death to bring life again.

Yes birth brings forth joy but with that joy comes some pain, ask any mother. We bring forth in pain because we are born in sin and we go through pain in Christ because we are born again to win. What Jesus felt for us was real! It's time we be real with ourselves and God. Nothing in this life is worth more than a life hid in Christ

God wants a people that will serve Him in Spirit and in Truth. He wants a people that will put Him first. He wants a people that will be willing to die for the Gospel sake. We have to take what life we live in Christ. This way has been fought against the entire life of man; from Adam until now.

THE BUILT UP SOUL

The Cares of Life Chokes Man

Because of the cares of this life God has been denied and rejected by the earth's inhabitants

Jeremiah 6:19 hear O earth, behold I will bring evil upon this people, even the fruit of their thought because they have not hearkened unto my words, nor my Law but rejected it.

Rejected means one has been refused, agreed with, used or believed. It means one has been discarded or thrown out as worthless, useless, or substandard; cast off or cast out. They are passed over or skipped without ever being given a thought to. They have been rebuffed, denied acceptance, care or love. It means we have declined God..

Genesis 6:5-12 God saw the wickedness of man that it was great in the earth, the imagination of the thoughts of man's heart was evil continually and it repented the Lord that he had made man on the earth and it grieved him to his heart. Man make God sick, nearly giving Him a heart attack but God said he would destroy man who he had created from the face of the earth.

But Noah, one man found grace in the eyes of God. The earth was filled with violence and was corrupt for all flesh had corrupted his way upon the earth.

Can't we see just as then man has corrupted the earth as then. ***Genesis 6:13 God told Noah the end of all flesh is come before me, for the earth is filled with violence through man, and behold I will destroy them with the earth.***

In ***Genesis 8:21*** the Lord said in his heart, I will not again curse the ground anymore for man's sake; for the imagination of man's heart is evil from his youth. Man is so depraved; yet they reject God who has all things including us in his hands.

THE BUILT UP SOUL

Job said in **Job 15:14** what is man that he should be clean? And he which is born of a woman, that he should be righteous? God created and made man clean in the beginning. They were created and made in righteousness as He.

Man put no trust in Saints, and heaven is not clean in the sight of men. How much more abominable and filthy is man which drink iniquity like water? But man says in his heart there is no God. Man lives, do and say corrupt things.

There works are done in abomination; great hatred and disgust, they dislike what is required of them to do very much but for whatever the reason they do it anyway no matter how vile. Man is found everyday doing things that are nasty and disgusting; highly unpleasant. The things they do are things they have no agreement with and are in bad taste.

An abominable thing is something very hateful. A prostitute hates what they do but for the money that they think answer all their need they will do it. Its loathsome to them; they are unwilling, reluctant, and hostile to doing it.

Soon man stopped seeking God or desiring to understand. Man have all gone together to go aside from God's ways. They have all together become filthy, there is none that do good, not one (**Ps. 53:1-3**). David said in **Psalm 53:5 behold I was shapen in iniquity and in sin di my mother conceive me**.

Solomon said in **Ecclesiastes 7:20** there is not a just man upon earth that doeth good, and sinneth not. He said that he found out (**Eccl. 7:29**) that God hath made man upright but they have sought out many inventions. They will not fear God to walk in his ways, nor will they turn their heart to God.

THE BUILT UP SOUL

Ecclesiastes 9:3 the heart of the sons of men is full of evil and madness is in their hearts while they live. We are as an unclean thing although God made all things clean. *Isaiah 64:6 all of our righteousness are as filthy rags*.

Jeremiah 13:23 can the Ethiopian change his skin or the leopard his spots? No! So then they that does do good can if they not become accustomed to doing evil. Don't practice doing wrong; delight yourself in righteousness that can only come through a life with Christ.

The heart is deceitful above all things and desperately wicked (*Jer. 17:9*). God sent his Son Jesus that died for the sins of men. God took Jesus blood and once for all sprinkled it upon us covering our sin that we be once again clean from all filthiness of the flesh.

Jesus dying brought to man once again; a new heart and he put a new spirit within us. He took out the stony heart which lieth in our flesh and gave us a heart of flesh that could be massaged with love and righteousness.

A good man out of the good treasure of the heart brings forth good things. We choose good or evil. Because man's deeds are evil by their choice they reject the light that came to them.

Because they reject Jesus they are condemned of their own doing. Because they reject Jesus they reject God and are carnal. We find among carnal men envying, strife, and divisions.

There is no agreement but bitterness and confusion bringing forth murders and corruptness. They live in the bond of iniquity. Division is birth forth.

In *Jeremiah 6:19* we find that the people had gone far away from God as they once had in Noah's time. Jeremiah is sometime spoken of as the most interesting

THE BUILT UP SOUL

prophetic figure in the "Old Testament" because he was the most Christian of all the prophets.

One author speaks of him as "most Christlike" of all; another as the healthiest, strongest, and bravest, grandest man of Old Testament history. He watched the decline and fall of man's relationship with God doing his time.

Jeremiah was called to be a prophet at a very tender age. He was sent by God to speak to Judah but also to the nations. God still call us as young as the womb.

He was bidden to remain un-married, hence he knew no family joys or consolations. He was exceedingly human and very sensitive, a true patriot, though full of complaints against both his people and society. We can't agree with things that go against God.

We find today that man has not changed from Jeremiah or Noah's time. The subject of sin has not changed and the change of disease in the nation has not changed. The Church has changed to the world in this time we live in. God forbid!

Jeremiah spent most of his time rebuking men for forsaking God, their idolatry, skepticism and unbelief, immortality, blind formalism, self-confidence and obduracy (hardheartedness).

They were hardhearted, would not change, wouldn't repent their sins, were stubborn and wouldn't give over to God's Law. They were like men today; inflexible to change. Jeremiah consistently preached in an age of change, convulsion and revolution. Jerusalem was going through her death agonies.

It was a period of hardness, obstinacy (stubbornness, resistant to change) and apathy (lack of emotion, interest, and unconcerned).

THE BUILT UP SOUL

The people lived to displease God! Vices and injustice of all kinds were frequently or commonly occurring and was widespread. Idolatry, unbelief, ceremony, rituals, disregard of equality and honor was widespread.

Immortality and Licentiousness (disregarding accepted rules and standards; morally unrestrained especially in sexual activity, lascivious) ravished the land at this time; so as it is in today's society.

The people had a license to sin; pretty much like today. If an act is right and proper why would one have to fight for approval of it?

If man have to approve a lifestyle by making it a law that goes against God's command or ordained order it's not alright. God is not pleased with such laws.

At the day of Jeremiah there was no justice, nor purity, nor integrity, nor nobleness of purpose in the land. Does this seem to address us today? There is today as then murder, perjury and theft abounding everywhere.

Conditions kept growing worse and worse; the nations was sliding lower and lower, over the precipice (a greatly hazardous situation, verging on disaster) of national ruin.

The activity within this nation that most are not yet conscious of immediately its impact upon with God can be recalled as publicly as it was announced. The people of the world today as then; have rapidly become totally careless and godless in their living and know they are wrong.

Lifestyles were just as stormy then as they are now. Does the Church today labor in vain? Since Jeremiah's day man has successfully seemingly to exert the power of influence negatively in the world in that they reigns the material over the spiritual and the physical over the moral doing what is wrong at any cost.

159

THE BUILT UP SOUL

We are warned to be Christ like but it is a choice every man living must make themselves. We have been given a new covenant in that man couldn't live the old covenant in that it could not secure that man should keep it.

A new covenant was needed not a new law. Men today still make laws to govern men sin that they don't live according to the New Covenant.

The law under the New Covenant was to be written on men hearts, so the New Covenant is spiritual; it's an inside job. Obedience to it will be a spiritual instinct, not doing what comes natural.

The Old Covenant given to Moses was written on tables of stone and only made demands; the New Covenant being Spiritual was sanctioned from within.

The difference between the two covenants is not one of chronology but the difference between law and religion, between the letter and the Spirit.

Religion is conceived as redemption from sin, but it is relationship with God that is drawing man near Him. Today man as then live under the Law of the land rather than God's spiritual law that brought us in relationship to Him.

We have rejected God and creation where He brought the world and everything therein into existence.

God as Creator has been rejected by the earth's inhabitants. God is the Creator and Maker of all things. Man rejects their Maker every day that they reject the fact that they are who they are and what they are. We are not to lay up treasures for ourselves in the earth but in heaven for where our treasure is so will our heart be (*Matt. 6:19*).

160

THE BUILT UP SOUL

Man must learn to be content with having what they are in need of more than their wants. These people of Jerusalem were given to covetousness according to **Jeremiah 6:13** from the least of them even to the greatest of all them.

Covetous is being greedy, longing for with envy what belongs to another.

Paul in **Colossian 3:2** tells us to set our affection on things above, not on things on the earth.

Jude 11 says woe unto them for they have gone in the way of Cain, and ran greedily after the error of Balaam for reward, and perished in the gainsaying of Core.

THE BUILT UP SOUL

What Are We Saying To Our Soul

Luke 12:19 and I will say to my soul, thou have much goods laid up for many years; take thine ease, eat, drink, and be merry.

It's time we the people of God tell Satan to get back off of us; we not together! We are together with God and God is looking for the faithful! God is concerned about our faithfulness to Him.

We confessed Christ, changed our walk and talk but what about our faithfulness and us being faithful to the promise, plan, and work of God? Where does our integrity lie? Where is our commitment taking us? What is our allegiance pledged to? Where?

Jesus spoke this parable in Luke in answer to the man that was worrying about his brother halfing up the inheritance left him. We will one day give an account to God for our soul.

Luke 12:20 but God said to him, thou fool, this night thy soul shall be required of thee; then whose shall those things be, which thou has provided?

Have we really considered the things in earth doesn't really mean much if God isn't using them in our lives for his glory? We need to back up off that which have no purpose for God. We must deny treasure given us that separates us from God.

Many children are mistreated and abused because of the meanness of grown folks that only seek a dollar bill come into their hand. They store up treasure to themselves and its not *"rich toward God"* (*Luke 12:21*).

When God gets ready to bless someone He considers their faithfulness to his service. Are we hungry for Him,

THE BUILT UP SOUL

His Word, and His Spirit? If not let's get hungry so we can learn to be faithful to the things of God.

Proverbs 20:6 most men will proclaim everyone his own goodness but a faithful man who can find?

Proverbs 28:20 a faithful man shall abound with blessings.

Man's soul as does God requires we be faithful. Being faithful means the revealed truth we believe in is; exhibited in our lives loyally and truthfully. It means we can be trusted with what God has put in us; we are honest and walk upright before God and man.

Our belief in God and the Scriptures are first in our lives for this is the very reason we live. Faithful means we put first things first, keeping fast our belief in God, holding our allegiance to Him by having a strong sense of duty or responsibility.

When we are faithful we learn of God and become conscientious of our devotion. Our attention to the things of God changes, we become more aware of how much God relies on us to do what He say and know to do that is right.

God wants our devotion and looks to see if we are dependable. Can He put his work in our hands and know that we will carry out what He has called us to do. He wants to know if He put anything in our hand we will handle it right.

THE BUILT UP SOUL

Walk In Faithfulness

Faithfulness is the quality of being faithful, loyalty, constancy, and fidelity. A faithful man who is reliable, consistent, steady, committed and dependable God will commit things in their hands. Can we be trusted like that? When God can trust us it means we are valuable to Him.

We can't be like the yo-yo the kids play with; up today and down tomorrow not knowing which way we take or why. Faithful people are friendly and hard to find among the elite of the world.

We must proclaim faithfulness, confess it, hear it and know what it is. Be strong in the grace of Christ for it will help the faithful to be strong. Faithfulness helps us succeed; those things we have heard and learned we are to do to the best of our; ability. Faithful means we are healthy and abound in blessings.

When one is faithful they aren't easily turned around from the things of God. They aren't cast to and fro by every wind of doctrine. They don't trust in vain persons and their genealogies; for they aren't worth our time, money, or energy. When is enough, enough? God is expecting us to continually and faithfully do the work of God.

The faithful are the true believers. They are the loyal adherents or supporters of the work of Christ. Faithful implies steadfast adherence to a person or thing to which one is bound as by an oath or obligation.

We as the people of God are bound to the morals He has presented in His Holy Word that we must live by. We are to be faithful to support and defend the Word. Our allegiance must be undeviating as God is; He does not change, He is immutable.

164

THE BUILT UP SOUL

People change, times change and circumstances change but God does not, will not and cannot.

If we say we love God we must be constant in our walk; free from fickleness in affections or loyalties. We stand strong in our principles and purpose. We are not easily turned aside by any cause but will defend the truth.

Not only that; but the faithful are resolute, having an unwavering determination in adhering to the personal relationship between them and God to nurture it.

Brains that can't think; follow not after them. We must make up our minds to follow God and be faithful no matter who else quits. Everything the saved, sanctified, Holy Ghost filled believer does must first be done as to the Lord.

If we do things unto the Lord we aren't so easily ready to allow feelings to play a part. Feelings have no part in the life of the faithful; we move with God. We obey because He is God. We follow on to know God so we learn to follow instructions. Being faithful to God means sometime we have to tell it like it is. We must do what God says.

Being faithful to God means we don't take sides against the anointed nor speak foolishly about them. If we want to abound in blessings keep the man of God out of your mouth. Foolish talking forces faithfulness out. We must lead by example; do what God calls us to.

In God's kingdom the least is the greatest and even the minute part of ministry is just as important. Whoever comes in and clean the bathroom is just as important as the Deacon or Missionary that collects the offering. When someone comes to visit and the bathroom is dirty they are likely not coming back.

If no one sets the clock or buy new batteries for the clock how can we start services on time? We can't if we don't

THE BUILT UP SOUL

know the time. No one is as important as the next when it comes to God and faithfulness. Everybody have their part; just have peace in doing yours.

Faithfulness has an excitement that goes along with it. We must be excited about what we do for Christ and do it faithfully. When we do what God has called us to do we have a peace about doing it and it brings joy our way.

Every man will give an account to God for what we have done in the earth; will we be found faithful? We must be faithful to our purpose, call and appointments. We must be faithful to leadership and authority. We must be faithful to God; He is concerned!

THE BUILT UP SOUL

If We Can Just Believe

What does it mean to believe? Believe means we trust, accept, and think that what we find trustworthy, creditable, and convincing is true. We convert, adhere and follow that which we believe.

On the Cross at Calvary we find our beloved Jesus; one loved and adored by many that worshipped, idolized, treasured and favored Him. But yet there were two sinners hung with Him on each side. Jesus was caught up in the middle of two thieves; a symbolism of sin. One of the thieves believed and the other did not.

In **Matthew 27:19-24** during the sentencing of Jesus Pilate was caught up in the middle between Jesus and the people. Being warned by his wife that Jesus was a just man he washed his hands of the blood before the multitude. Although he released Jesus after scourging him to be crucified his heart was not in putting him to death.

Luke 17:34-36 lets us know that when Jesus come again two men will be in the bed; one will be taken and one left. Two women shall be grinding together; the one shall be taken and the other left. Two men shall be in the field, the one shall be taken, and the other left.

Jesus is caught up in the middle of our decision to choose righteousness over sin because He died for our sin that we may have life eternal. Jesus is the referee between God and Satan for the souls of men. He will judge us according to the Word.

We must learn to refrain from sin. We should avoid sin and cease from anger. Not only that but we have been commanded to abstain from things that is not ordained by God. We are to have some forbearance when it comes to the crossroads of life as Jesus did.

167

THE BUILT UP SOUL

In replenishing our lives with the invigorating Word of God we renew our relationship with our heavenly Father and we can take refuge in the center of His will. This refuge point is in the middle of decisions rather we know it or not. How well we are protected from the hands of the enemy depends on how well we obey God's Word and how well we walk in regard to His Ways.

We are put on notice that we mark ourselves by the way we view and think while we are caught in the middle of controversy with the Devil.

We must respect the value of the Word and admire the leading of the Holy Spirit as well as esteeming God in the highest regard. We are to look with the highest estimation, appreciation, affection and admiration as we gaze through the looking glass and see God that we rely not on opinions but truth of the Word.

As the thief on the cross with Jesus looked on the Word and recognized that the man on the Cross in the middle was not a mere man. His estimation of who Jesus was took him to heaven that day. He found the Lord the day of his death. His appreciation of who Jesus was also established a verifiable, authenticated, and confirmed belief in Christ.

This newfound affection and admiration secured him a fixed stabilized position with not only Jesus but God. Jesus that day fulfilled the thief's euphoria, well-being and happiness. Jesus was the center of the thief's heart, mind, soul, and spirit. We can believe that this man's countenance was one of approval as he was approved of by the Son of God.

He went to the cross as a sinner but was acknowledged by Jesus as going to Paradise with Him as a saved man. Jesus position in the middle is to make intercession for us that we may endure and continue in our belief and trust in Him.

THE BUILT UP SOUL

The race is not to the swift; nor to the strong but to them that endure to the end. We must endure suffering and persecution with fortitude, tolerance, perseverance and stamina. We will be like a rock when Jesus is caught up in the middle of our lives.

We are rooted, established, and grounded in Holiness. Our hearts are fixed and based firmly. Christ wants to be instituted, erected, and built up in and through us. With Him comes an assembly, a group arranged and classified as one with God.

This group the Father, the Son, and the Holy Ghost that worked together in the Creation to make us that spiritual being that we were created to be wants to be caught up in the middle of every one of our lives.

How do we do this? Through repentance, sanctification, and holiness which is the first state of man's spirituality and being. God wants us to know that He is the Lord that sanctifies us; He formed us and knew us before we came forth out of our mother's womb.

Jesus prayed in **John 17:17** to the Father to sanctify us through His Truth; His Word is Truth. Jesus for our sakes sanctified himself that we also might be sanctified through the truth. He was caught up in the middle for us that we would open our eyes to turn them from darkness to light and from the power of Satan unto God that we may receive forgiveness of sins and inheritance among them which are sanctified by faith that is in Christ Jesus. We are called to be Saints sanctified in Christ Jesus.

What do we receive for sainthood in Christ Jesus? We receive that same wisdom, righteousness, sanctification, and redemption after we have been washed in the blood of Jesus Christ. We accordingly have been chosen before the Creation to be holy and without blame before Him in love.

THE BUILT UP SOUL

We are to know the love of Christ which passes knowledge, that we might be once again filled with all the fullness of God. Jesus is caught up in the middle to help us know how to possess our vessels in sanctification and honor that our whole spirit, soul, and body be preserved blameless unto His coming again.

God has from the beginning chosen us to salvation through sanctification of the Spirit and belief of the truth. We are to purge ourselves that we may be meat for the master's use and prepared unto every good work. Jesus caught up in the middle sanctified, sanctifies us and all of us are one with Christ. He offered up His body once for all.

For by one offering He has perfected forever them that are sanctified that we may be partakers of God's Holiness. He according to His divine power has given unto us all things that pertain unto life and godliness through the knowledge of him that hath called us to glory and virtue that we may be a partaker of the divine nature, having escaped the corruption that is in the world through lusts. What more can He do?

If we confess our sins, He is faithful and just to forgive us our sins, and to cleanse us from all unrighteousness. He is able to keep us from falling and to present us faultless before the presence of His glory with exceeding joy.

Will you be one today that will come out of great tribulation as Jesus did and have your robe washed and made white in the blood of the Lamb? Will you be as Jesus was willing to be caught up in the middle?

I, one day found Jesus and the sin of the past is gone. The sins committed against me is forgiven. A new life in Christ I found and there is no greater love and joy I have found. God through Christ his Word restored me with my mother after I prayed and believed. There is restoration to everyone that will believe and trust in God. I know without a doubt that it was God that have saved me!

THE BUILT UP SOUL

Saved By Grace For Eternal Life

We have been given Salvation; something that Satan can never and will never have! We have been adopted in the Kingdom of God. *I Peter 2:9* says we are a chosen people, a royal priesthood, a holy nation, a people belonging to God, that we may declare the praises of him who called us out of darkness into his wonderful light.

Ephesians 2:1-6 and you hath he quickened, who were dead in trespasses and sins; wherein in time past ye walked according to the course of this world, according to the prince of the power of the air, the spirit that now worketh in the children of disobedience; among whom also we all had our conversation in times past in the lusts of our flesh, fulfilling the desires of the flesh and of the mind; and were by nature the children of wrath, even as others. But God, who is rich in mercy for his great love wherewith he loved us, even when we were dead in sins, hath quickened us together with Christ, (by grace are ye saved;) and hath raised us up together and made us sit together in heavenly places in Christ Jesus.

Christ is our Redeemer, our Brother, and our Deliverer. He is the instrument of God's deliverance of mankind from sin. The day of the Lord is coming, the day of the last judgment and the end of the world. It is a day that God will punish evil.

Time and time again God warned us through his prophets of the day of the Lord. We have time and time again been warned to repent and turn to the Lord for there is life in Christ. This is God's grace; not giving us the death and judgment we deserve. Do we desire to see the day of the Lord? It is a day of darkness and not light. Except we be saved we shall perish.

THE BUILT UP SOUL

God knows our manifold transgressions and our mighty sins; we afflict the just, quick to take a bribe, and we turn aside the poor from their rights.

We are a people, Lord the help; that seek not the good but do evil continually. So why do we need grace you say? Why do we need to let the dead bury the dead and follow Jesus? Paul with unmistakable emphasis declares by grace are ye saved!

He dispels any notion that salvation is in any sense of ourselves and asserts its gratuitous character as a gift of God. There is left no doubt as to the cause of men's salvation. God alone affect the sinner's salvation not the sinner himself that may start it and God completes it or the sinner affects his salvation by his own efforts.

The sinner's salvation begins when they hear the Word, repents and confesses Christ, deny themselves and follow Christ. *Ephesian 2:8* for by grace are ye saved through faith; and that not of yourselves it is the gift of God.

It is made from the premise that man is dead in trespasses and sins, and a child of wrath by nature, therefore they are unable to help themselves out of their misery under sin.

What is this grace that saves the sinner? It is an affection in God which springs from his mercy, love, and kindness. This same righteous God who has a horror of sin, loves the sinner in spite of their sin with an active desire to reclaim him. This desire of God is saving grace; it always has sin for its correlate.

Saving grace exists in God together with His holiness and righteousness. The gospel proclaims God's saving grace made known to us in the mystery of His Will according to His good pleasure. Out of the same divine mind has come the stern law with its grievous injunctions and terrible doom and the sweet evangel of pardon and peace to sinners.

Saving grace then is never any quality in the sinner by which he propitiates God against whom he has sinned; it is never some virtue infused into the sinner by which the latter is enabled to procure his salvation; but it is always that remarkable disposition in God to be favorable to the sinner (the benign favor of God towards sinners) or (the gracious kindness which God bears towards us in His heart).

It is therefore utterly unmerited on the part of the sinner and cannot be purchased or brought at any other price than the one paid at Calvary by His Son.

God had decreed to save fallen man back in the eternal counsel long before our time. Christ effected the sinner's reconciliation with His Father. Saving grace embraces the entire evangelical plan of salvation from repentance over sin through conversion, justification, sanctification, preservation in faith, to glorification and lastly it embraces the means by which God communicates salvation to the sinner.

Before faith in Christ has been created in his heart man does not cooperate with the grace that is offered him according to *I Corinthians 2:14;* but the natural man receiveth not the things of the Spirit of God; for they are foolishness unto him; neither can he know them, because they are spiritually discerned.

Grace yet does not operate in an irresistible manner *Matthew 23:37* O Jerusalem, Jerusalem, thou that killest the prophets, and stonest them which are sent unto thee, how often would I have gathered thy children together, even as a hen gathereth her chickens unto her wings and ye would not!

THE BUILT UP SOUL

After the Gospel of grace however has won the heart by its persuasive power, he does work together with the Holy Spirit in the sanctification of his life however not of or by his own natural power but by the power of the new spiritual life which saving grace has created in him. It is God that is able to do abundantly above all that we ask or think, according to the power that works in us.

We that are saved are saved by grace. God told Paul in **II Corinthians 12:9** that his grace was sufficient for him for his strength is made perfect in weakness. The things we have the most problem with are the things that make us strong when we overcome them.

God doesn't always take things that bothers or buffets us away from us but uses them to bring us to a state of thankfulness. It reminds us that God is yet able. It reminds us that God's grace is sufficient for us. We then take pleasure in those things after we have come to realize that they aren't there to take us out but it makes us strong in the Lord.

We are saved by grace, converted; bear godly conduct and serving love, or their virtues and good works but this is not saving grace, but a manifestation of its presence and operation in believers; for otherwise salvation would be by works, which Scripture forbids in **Ephesians 2:8**.

Had not it been for God's grace we all would perish. Hell would have enlarged itself and Satan would have overthrown God. Had we been given the punishment due us for the sin we have done we would have built Satan's kingdom as he had planned.

God is our strength and song and he is become our salvation. He has loaded us with his benefits. Great is his mercy towards us for he has delivered our souls from the lowest hell. All the ends of the earth have seen the salvation of our God and yet not obey his Word; it's

THE BUILT UP SOUL

God's grace that has kept us all from being consumed in a smoke.

He reasons with us and though our sins are as scarlet they shall be as white as snow, though they are red like crimson they shall be as wool because of God's grace. Because of God's grace we too are saved like Israel with an everlasting salvation.

When we take his yoke upon us, bring all of our heaviness to Him, He will give us rest. We just need to make up our minds that we will endure all the way to the end for it is needful. Only they that endure to the end shall be saved.

Repentance and remission of sins brings us to worship and worship brings us to God. If we lift Him up from the earth He will draw all men to him. If we abide in him and He in us we will find all the help we need to run this race that is set before us. Without God we can do nothing; it is his saving grace that keeps us.

The Gospel of Christ is the power of God unto salvation which we cannot get around. Herein is the righteousness of God revealed from faith to faith for the just shall live by faith. We have to work out our own salvation and allow God's saving grace to work in and through us.

Jesus became the author of eternal salvation unto all of us that will obey Him. He was made perfect through all he went through for us. He makes intercession for us daily, he stands at the door of our hearts knocking, begging us to open up and let him come in for he wants to save us.

Grace is given freely and we can receive God's amazing grace in our own bosom. God's grace is there because it's not his will that any man perish.

The end will come when the Gospel has been preached all over the world to all men; men are baptized in the

THE BUILT UP SOUL

name of the Father and of the Son, and of the Holy
Ghost. All nations would have heard the Word and
sinners given a time of repentance!

Grace and repentance would have then been given to all
of mankind.

Whosoever hear the Word and believe it unto
repentance will have everlasting life. Jesus the Son of
man did not come to destroy our lives but to save them.

I John 1:1-2 that which was from the beginning, which
we have heard, which we have seen with our eyes,
which we have looked upon, and our hands have
handled, of the Word of life;

(For the life was manifested, and we have seen it, and
bear witness, and show unto you that eternal life, which
was with the Father, and was manifested unto us)

THE BUILT UP SOUL

Comfort Or Torment; We Choose

Life, eternal life is the life God promised man that they were to prepare for in the Earth. This preparation was for a return to our Heavenly home from whence we originally came.

Something is wrong; why is the world dying and accepting to go to an unprepared eternal resting place? Why would a man want to associate his Soul with Hell for Eternity when there is a mansion prepared for him in Heaven?

Does anyone wonder about Eternal life, evidently not when so many are dying such meaningless death?

Man was always promised eternal life, to live forever. What came between man living and ruling in this earth is the fact that he disobeyed his Creator.

God had created man with an eternal purpose. Satan still deceives man today with his half-truths. He takes just enough of truth to a situation to make his case seem like it is true.

Many have been deceived by his deceptive antics. No one can live like a Devil all of his life and expect to accept Christ on their dying bed and expect to receive the same reward as one that has loved, obeyed and lived for God throughout the process of their time of defilement and works.

Eternal life for man was an original plan of God from the beginning of creation, from the time that he breathed the breath of life in man and he became a living soul. This brought forth the union of the Soul and the Body and this coming together is what gave man Eternal Life. Eternal means existing always, essentially unchanging, everlasting, timeless, infinite, endless, limitless, immoral, invariable, permanent, fixed, constant, enduring, lasting, or everlasting in eternity.

THE BUILT UP SOUL

There is life after death for God's created beings, man and woman. In life they must make preparations to have that life. God has given them everything to sustain them in life, the capacity to grow, have functional activities, and the continued ability to change for the better until their departure in this natural life.

Eternal life is the always, existing union of soul and body. Life is considered the period between birth and death in a man's life. In times past man lived longer lives than that of today. In Genesis they had promise of one hundred twenty years and in Psalm David said man then had a promise of threescore and ten which was seventy years. Sin brought forth death and decay to the days of man in the earth.

Children today are more learned that men and women were then. They existed before Christ, but now these people living after Christ has the living Word that was manifested in the earth and there is no excuse for the sin of mankind.

We have the road map laid out in front of us and we do understand what is on the road and the sacrifices made and the choices given them for that road to exist. For our God and this is not to say or imply that everyone know Christ, why he came into the world, and why he died but, we do know that because he came from Heaven and dwell among men to show them a better way to live; they should accept his finished work of the Cross.

Man can be in obedience to the Father God which is in Heaven. Man has a reason to praise the Lord in the beauty of Holiness. His own individual actions and how they view Christ in their lives will cause them to miss out on God's promise of eternal life. They imprison themselves in the mind because of the sin that they try to hide there.

Man's choices lead them either to Christ or away from Christ; the pleasure of sin is deceiving in that it is only for

THE BUILT UP SOUL

that moment. The Christian must be careful not to listen to the enemy too long. When Satan brings accusations on ourselves or on our sisters and brothers in Christ, we listen to a half- truth.

Man need to arise out of that state that they become inactive in because they have assumed an imaginary animation of what another Christian is or is not doing. Wrong answer, they will miss Heaven. Holiness is right and somebody is wrong, man cannot do what they may want to and go to Heaven.

We must purge the sin that so easily besets them time and time again. Life is existence, being, sentience, viability, lifetime, days, efficacy, mortal human being, individual, soul, living and way of life, lifestyle, and passions.

Our new saved life in Christ affords us grace but it's not to be misused or taken for granted. Habitually taking advantage of the grace we have been given will cause us to miss heaven and abort eternal life. We have been saved by grace for eternal life.

THE BUILT UP SOUL

Pulling Down Strongholds In Us

II Corinthians 10:3-4 for though we walk in the flesh; we do not war after the flesh; (for the weapons of our warfare are not carnal, but mighty to the pulling down of strongholds). Paul said we must cast down everything that exalts itself against the knowledge of God and bring into captivity every thought to the obedience of Christ. Our problem in this life is we have to deal with our mind, our thoughts, our heartfelt emotions and our will.

We are our own worst enemy. We have our own agenda when we should be doing what God requires of us. We have become mass weapons of destruction to ourselves. We have succeeded in destroying mass areas in the life of man where Christ is concerned because we don't realize the weapon God has put in our hands is greater than any earthly weapon man can create.

For what reason do we live? Why were we created and made? God had a purpose for each and every one of us. When we find that purpose we will make our lives complete. We will find ourselves submitting to the Word, Will, and Purpose of God for our lives.

I Thessalonians 5:23 the very God of peace sanctify you wholly; and I pray God your whole spirit and soul and body be preserved blameless unto the coming of our Lord Jesus Christ.

It is God that has made us and not we; our self. God wants us to be totally healed, delivered, and set free from all that will come to oppress us but there are things we must do and follow.

Deuteronomy 28:2 and all these blessings shall come upon thee and overtake thee, if thou shall hearken unto the voice of the Lord thy God. We must hide the Word of God in our heart that we "sin not against Him. The biggest fight man have is the one within himself to submit to God's Word.

THE BUILT UP SOUL

The Bible is a record of God's self-revelation. In and through such experience God was revealing Himself to us. We find the most vital and significant truths about God. God is intelligent and powerful and a great lover of beauty. God comforts our needy hearts and answers our deepest questions or stir us to live on the highest moral plane. If we read the Bible, study it, meditate on the Word therein we will find God.

We will learn the full meaning of our sin and the gracious provision God has made whereby we sinners may find forgiveness and restoration to divine fellowship. When we bear in mind that the purpose of the Bible is to reveal God, we have no trouble appreciating why the Book is quite unconcerned about some matters in which modern men have an eager interest.

God work in stages in revealing himself to us; we could not contain all of Him all at once. We go through stages in our spiritual walk but it is solely for God's purpose. Through the Bible there is a thread of divine purpose which gives unity to the entire volume.

That purpose is redemption, finding its fulfillment and realization in Jesus Christ. It deals with the basic issues of human living and is a trustworthy guide for the believer to believe about God, sin, salvation, about life here and hereafter. We find dependable answers there. The same Holy Spirit works today as worked then. He takes the message and the events and makes them live with meaning for us in our particular life situations. We will be inspired by God as we are not independent to God as intellectual beings, but for small and great, old and young alike.

It is the inspiration of God that gives us understanding. In *II Timothy 3:16* the expression *given by inspiration of God* is used in its more proper and specific sense as a direct predicate of the written Scriptures, affirming that quality of divinity in them by virtue of which they are profitable for the great ends for which they are given.

THE BUILT UP SOUL

In the life of the believer the Bible is our divine source of inspiration. The words which the prophets of old spoke from the Lord to the Israel inspired them to go on with the Lord. We are inspired by the Holy Ghost today for He will give us in the same hour what we ought to say or do.

Why do we rely on the Scripture as our inspiration for right living? All Scripture is given by inspiration of God and is profitable for doctrine, for reproof, for correction, for instruction in righteousness.

We live stable in Christ Jesus. Stability comes and we don't meddle with stuff we should not be a part of that is given to change. No longer do we wander for we know our places. No man can serve two masters for either we will hate one and love the other or else we will hold the one and despise the other but not both.

When our hearts are established with grace we are not carried about with divers and strange doctrines. We ask of God things in faith, nothing wavering for a double minded man is unstable in all his ways. Because of the stability we have grown in and come to know in Christ we build integrity. We become able to do all that God has called us to do.

We have purpose. Our tongue will not speak wickedness nor our tongues utter deceit. Righteousness will be held close and we will not let our heart reproach us. We weigh things in an even balance that God may know our integrity for which he will judge us by along with our righteousness.

We will understand the fear of the Lord and find the knowledge of God when we apply our heart to understanding and our ear to wisdom. We are solely for God's purpose. It is God's purpose that we let not mercy and truth forsake us. We are to bind them about our neck, write them on the table of our heart.

THE BUILT UP SOUL

When we apply God to every purpose and plan we find favor and good understanding in the sight of God and man. We are children of God covered by the blood of Jesus.

Romans 8:16-17 the Spirit itself beareth witness with our spirit, that we are the children of God; and if children, then heirs; heirs of God, and joint-heirs with Christ; if so be that we suffer with him, that we may be also glorified together.

I Peter1:18-21 forasmuch as ye know that ye were not redeemed with corruptible things, as silver and gold, from your vain conversation received by tradition from your fathers; but with the precious blood of Christ, as a lamb without blemish and without spot; who verily was foreordained before the foundation of the world, but was manifest in these last times for you, who by him do believe in God, that raised him up from the dead, and gave him glory; that your faith and hope might be in God.

Children are special, we are special. Children naturally are considered young persons of either sex. We are what we are when we are born, male or female; boy or girl. But when we are born again and become a Christian, meaning we are Christ like we must put on some things other than clothes. We must wear the covering of the blood of Christ.

Jesus said in *Matthew 18:3* except we be converted and become as little children, ye shall not enter into the kingdom of heaven. We are not to be forbidden to come to Him for there we find the kingdom of heaven.

A child is known by his doings whether they are pure and right or playful and wrong. We too will be known for our deeds whether they are for or of Christ. The counsel of a man's heart runs deep   like a river of deep water but when he understands his way he will love the way he takes. If we are children of God we love the way we take

183

or if we are sinners we love the way we take. Whatever it is that we do we should take pleasure in it.

The just man walks in his integrity. A king scatters away evil with his eyes; everyone comes into subjection when he enters his throne. So much more Christ when he sits on the throne of our hearts we should fear what we do that we do; that it is what is right in the sight of God.

Death and life are in the power of the tongue. As Children of God we learn to speak what the Word says. We learn to say what God says about us and our situations. We learn to speak life to dead situations.

Isaiah 9:6 for unto us a child is born, unto us a son is given; and the government shall be upon his shoulder; and his name shall be called Wonderful, Counselor, The mighty God, the Everlasting Father, The Prince of Peace. Isaiah was speaking of the child Jesus that would come and make us children of God once again.

We are to be Spirit led, Spirit filled, and Spirit controlled. Children receive the DNA of their father. We are Christians and have received the DNA of God. Therefore brethren, we are debtors, not to the flesh, to live after the flesh. For if ye live after the flesh, ye shall die; but if ye through the Spirit do mortify the deed of the body, ye shall live.

For as many as are led by the Spirit of God, they are the sons of God *Romans 8:12-14*. We are followers of Christ and were first called Christians at Antioch in *Acts 11:26*.

To be the children God calls us to be we must delight in the Law of God. How do we do this? We must realize that sanctification and holiness is an inside job and manifest on the outside.

The Children of God must allow a transformation to take place in the heart; we need a heart transplant. We need

THE BUILT UP SOUL

the new blood flowing through us that Jesus shed on the Cross for us; that life giving blood. According to Luke we have a new covenant in **Luke 22:20** this cup is the New Testament in my blood which is shed for us. This covers the whole body through the process of redemption **Ephesians 1:7** in whom we have redemption through his blood, the forgiveness of sins, according to the riches of his grace.

We are given all that God is through Christ Jesus; hope that is laid up in heaven, the Word of the truth of the Gospel, the fruit that the Word brings forth, grace, love in the Spirit, the knowledge of his Will in all wisdom and spiritual understanding, strengthened with all might, patience and longsuffering with joyfulness.

Now we can walk worthy of the Lord unto all pleasing, being fruitful in every good work and increasing the knowledge of God. God has made us meet to be partakers of the inheritance of the saints in light delivering us from the power of darkness and translating us into the kingdom of his dear Son.

He is the image of the invisible God, the firstborn of every creature; for by him were all things created, that are in heaven and that are in earth, visible and invisible, whether they be thrones, or dominions or principalities, or powers; created by him and for him; and he is before all things and by him all things consist. Jesus the head of the body will have all preeminence.

The blood of Jesus cleanses and makes us whole. It gives new life to dead stuff for it makes life whole with life giving fluid which make us live right. The natural body lives as long as there is blood flow. The precious blood of Jesus Christ makes life brand new that changes us forever.

It only takes one touch from the Master. In **Mark 5:25-29 There was a certain woman which had an issue of blood twelve years and had suffered many things of** many ***physicians, and had spent all that she had, and was nothing bettered, but rather grew worse. When she had heard of Jesus, came in the press behind, and touched his garment. For she said, if I may touch but his clothes I shall be whole and straightway the fountain of her blood was dried up; and she felt in her body that she was healed of that plague.***

We are the Children of God and the blood of Jesus is there for us too. When we touch Him and it's the touch of faith we cause a change to come about in our situations; for God will move.

Heirs are someone that inherits or is entitled to inherit something upon the death of someone else by will or by law. They are someone that appears to get some trait from, or carry on in the tradition of, a predecessor. We are Christ predecessors and we are to carry on in his name the work he began in the earth. Jesus died leaving us an heir-ship that cannot be denied.

We cannot be denied salvation for it is ours for the asking for God has made it available to us. We are heirs that have a right to all that God through Jesus Christ has left here for us. We are children of God covered by the blood of Jesus with a promise from God to Abraham and all his descendants that we can expect to have a better life.

This is the inheritance God gave us; Christ Jesus. We are joined with God through the promise of Abraham and work of Christ Jesus so we are joint heirs. We have been doubled in. Christ is the heir of all things as being the Son of God. ***God who at sundry times and in divers manners spoke in time past unto the fathers by the prophets, hath in these last days spoken unto us by his Son, whom he that appointed heir of all things, by whom also he made the worlds; Hebrews 1:2.***

THE BUILT UP SOUL

A saved person is referred to as an heir of God through Christ according to **Galatians 4:7 wherefore thou art no more a servant, but a son; and if a son then an heir of God through Christ**. God has made known unto us as his children through the Spirit all mysteries concerning Christ which was not made to our forefathers.

Being adopted we are fellow-heirs with the Jews and are partakers of the same body and promise in Christ.

It's a perfect day in my life because I have found Christ; He is that peace in this life I so adoringly needed. I have learned Christ and knowing Him helps me to forgive and maneuver the terrains of this life day by day with joy.

Coming in relationship with the Father, through his darling Son Jesus and His precious Holy Spirit has taught me the real essence of who I am and how important my life lived for Christ really is in this time in my life!

I have pulled down the strongholds in my life. Now it's a perfect day, a new day, a most precious day that I rejoice in! Praise God, just stay the course

THE BUILT UP SOUL

Religion Or Relationship

Single, Marriage, Separation, Divorce, and Remarriage defines some part of man's life in the earth. It touches some part of religion and spelled out relationships.

Adam was first single with God. Adam and Eve were married to God in Spirit after God made bodies and put them in. They knew nothing else. But in their doings they found themselves separated from God because they disobeyed the one thing he forbid them to do.

Now that separation brought forth a death to the Spirit of God that reigned in them. Now they were tossed out of the Garden of Eden; God divorced them and they are strangers sojourning in an unknown place all alone.

They were left off to a state of widowhood; alone. Man had lost their place. They lost their way. They were confused. Satan had the victory he thought; but God had a plan to bring the relationship between he and man.

What is it we have; Religion or Relationship? We should be called because of a constant, persistent prayer life; Closet Freaks, Hit the closet; the prayer place we go to seek God which makes for proper relationship and order He calls us too. Prayer calls for a willing participation from us all; a separation to God alone, away from others.....

We can be First Class Citizens of Heaven in earth. In The Army Of God....how we see some things depends on which eyes we are seeing through, the

THE BUILT UP SOUL

left or the right....one eye may magnify what's there and the other eye don't see it at all.

Times and Seasons brings on the last hour, know the seasons of our life...the lunatick, the devil is a disaster waiting to happen; he is there to distract us from God's purpose and ordained Order in life. He is a mean, evil, defeated foe, but is no match for God; for he lost his place in God's heart .....he wants to be the headmaster in the life of man.

Satan knows though that God is the Lord and Master! He seeks to make us deny God, self and loved ones. He lies, steals and kill man's relationship with The Master; God!

God fills us with all the spiritual enrichment we need; expect Him to do something great in and through us ....We are building relationship with God on a daily basis! Our relationship with Him through the Word grows to maturity... The Word builds us up; for we believe that their is one Lord one Faith, one Baptism....if we will be saved its by the Word of God.....

We get the wisdom of God, we gain knowledge of Him and acquire the understanding that we may properly assert it to our heart that we can celebrate God and live the Gospel righteously; right now!!!!!!!!

THE BUILT UP SOUL

It Takes A Turning

God called man as his own, in his image and likeness to have dominion in the earth. God has given with his dominion some do's and don'ts. To make a turn mean we enact a difference in the way we do things where we cause a rotation or change to come about. We cause a revolving to take place where we change the direction we take.

God directs us through his Word and leads us through his Spirit ruling and reigning in our life. God sent his Son, Jesus to point us in the direction back to his Father as Lord and Creator of all things, **John 1:14.** Man's movement takes him away sometime; from God because we have moved out of position. God has given us an ordained well rounded purpose in Him.

Sometime our own way have to suffer an upset that we set our focus where it need to be. God has given man a central thought and place to be in life. We sometime need to do a circular motion away from the path we are following. If we expect to stay in God's grace we must do some things we think is not necessary. Our actions must be guarded. It takes a turning away from the norm sometime.

Putting a difference between clean and unclean, holy and unholy mean we upset or unsettle some people. We have to get to a place where its all about God. No matter what we see, do, or say it's a reflection on God. We must bend the course of sin where it is deflected and diverted in our life. God's Word on the inside of our heart must resonate to the outside where others see God glowing in our life.

THE BUILT UP SOUL

The knowledge we have received must take front and center, making plain what God has said. We ponder things in our minds that God has already said do or don't do. Why do we have to figure out what God has already said do or don't do? We already know we aren't to bend, fold or twist, or we should know anyway. Why do we constantly bend backwards when we know we can possibly break our back?

Jesus was sent, yes! He came to change man's condition in nature. We were a people most miserable caught up in a whirlwind of sin. We had to be changed, converted, and transmuted, meaning our nature and make up in life had to be completely turned around. What have we exchanged our soul for? What have we subjected our self to that left God out?

Satan has presented or translated to man another life outside of the confines of God. He makes every sweet thing bitter and every bitter thing sweet. He lies to, steals from, kills and destroy man's dreams and visions. He translate every thing God says to deceive man into being doubtful where God is concerned. He is one most ridiculed and tries subjecting us to ridicule.

Satan is the father of lies, distraction. He lures us away from God by means of pure deception that we be affected in some way. He love making God the most hated being in the world. That keep one bound in the confines of their own mind where they go against God. It keeps one going around in circles where we are not fully conscience of our proper directions.

THE BUILT UP SOUL

It takes a turning! We must turn our life around where we work on those things which is of sound doctrine. Those things that gives life. We can't partly do anything. All we do must be done with the strictest soundness. We can't effect change if we aren't changed. We can't seem to be something if we are not that. To put a monkey face or mask on does not make us a monkey.

Its time to stop being dizzy concerning life; either we are in or we are not. Either we will be saved or not saved. Either we are in Christ or not. Either we believe God or we don't. it takes a turning on our part. Many are being reeled in, into sin. They are giddy and dizzy concerning God. Yet we are without excuse for sin.

Man change and color their hair to make a point no matter how ugly it is. They shift and twist the body making it pretty ridiculous in the eyes of others but they get the attention they desire from it; what more then should we do to change for God?

It takes a turning! Anything worth having in life calls for some serious change sometime but we do it. what's important to us we make special effort for. We reverse our position to acquire that thing important to us. We will pay more money to go in a different direction if it will bring us to that desired place; how much more should we do in Christ?

Its time to take a different turn for God that our lives become more productive in Christ. Its time to stop deviating from the Word, the truth and God's Will, Way and Purpose.

We are called by God to be different, to make a difference. Its time to start moving in a direction

THE BUILT UP SOUL

away from sin to righteousness, from being unclean
in sin to clean in righteousness, and put a
difference between right and wrong.

It takes a turning. God has given to every man a
choice to accept Him or reject Him; we can't have it
both ways. Either we are for Him or against Him.

God is a Holy God that requires Holiness from man.
He looks for an action from man that calls for a
turning. Some things we must turn off, some roads
we can't go down. Some places we can't go. Some
people we must let go. Some music must be turned
off. Some things done must be undone.

We today must begin to reshape our lives to be
conformed to Christ through the Word, by the Spirit.

The choice is ours!

THE BUILT UP SOUL

Save Your Soul Alive

*Ezekiel 18:27-*28 again when the wicked man turns from the sin that is besetting him and do that which is lawful and right; he shall save his soul alive. Because he considered and turned away from all his transgressions that he had committed, he shall surely live; he shall not die.

The soul; why do we need to save our soul alive. Why is the soul important. The soul is that spiritual nature in man which is more than what is found in the Creation. It is spiritual, reasoning, and immortal The word soul is synonymous with the life of man.

*Leviticus 17:*11 for the life of the flesh is in the blood and I have given it to you upon the altar to make an atonement for your souls; for it is the blood that maketh atonement for the soul.

It would take a special sacrifice for man's soul to be saved in death. The law had a shadow of good things to come thereby sacrifices of the law and man was ineffective. The sacrifices man made for the sin done in their bodies year after year did not maintain a continual deliverance unto perfection.

According to Ezekiel in *Ezekiel 18:30-31* God said therefore I will judge you, O house of Israel, every one (the saved and sinner alike) according to his ways, said they Lord God, Repent and turn yourselves from all your transgressions; so iniquity shall not be your ruin. Cast away from you all your transgressions, whereby ye have transgressed; and make you a new heart and a new spirit, for why will ye die, O house of Israel?

THE BUILT UP SOUL

God has no pleasure in the death of one dying in sin. The *soul* **Ezekiel 18:20** says the soul that sinneth it shall die. Every man and woman shall bear the iniquity done in their own lives and not of another; father, mother, sister or brother, friend, husband or wife. A man's righteousness shall be upon him in like manner also.

So if we sin we will give an account for it after we have walked away from our righteousness. In like fashion if the wicked turns away from all his sins that he has committed and keep all the statutes of God and do that which is lawful and right; he shall live and not die. If we repent the sin and quit it, we shall live and not die.

When the righteous turns away from God as the Israelites did in Egypt, committing iniquity, hidden sin, doing all the abominations that the wicked man is doing, shall they escape the wrath of God? Shall he live? They lose the mention of the righteousness that they have done; for it shall not be accredited to them.

The trespass however, the sin committed will though be counted to him. He shall die in his sin, that he have sinned, **Ezekiel 18:24**. Man try laying charge of their sin either to another human or God.

We need a new mindset when it comes to God. God is not a man that He should lie, nor the son of man that he should lie. We can't serve sin in Christ. Our ways are not God's Way, nor our ways equal to God's Way. God is indeed fair in his Ways.

We the people in earth need to make that much needed change that we die not in sin. If we die in our sin its because we left off God and his righteousness without repenting, turning and quitting. When the wicked man turns from the sin that is besetting him and do that which is lawful and right; he shall save his soul alive.

Matthew 16:26 for what is a man profited if he shall gain the whole world and lose his own soul? Or what shall a man give in exchange for his soul?

Once we have been purged of sin, sacrifices should not continually have need to be offered. Once we have been purged, their should be no need for sacrifices; for the conscience of that desire for sin should also to have died.

Jesus said we must fit him in for He had come into the world as the only final sacrifice for sin. Animals have ceased to be offered.

David being confident in God hearing and answering his prayers cried out to God as Jesus of his lineage to come did, saying, I come in the volume of the book, it is written of me; where sacrifices and offerings for sin would not be required by God anymore.

Obedience is the best sacrifice; God requires it. This is the requirement Jesus brought with Him in redeeming the soul of man back from death. God requires man to come in obedience to his Word and Spirit that their soul lives eternally.

God requires man to come to Him in the righteousness of Christ that we have hope. We are to delight to do thy will, O my God, yea thy law is within my heart David said in *Psalms 40:8-10*, David said I have preached righteousness in the great congregation; lo I have not refrained my lips,

THE BUILT UP SOUL

O Lord, thou knowest. I have not hid thy righteousness within my heart but declared your faithfulness and salvation as Jesus would do also. He did not conceal God's loving kindness and truth from man. We too are required to do the same.

Romans 12:2 and be not conformed to this world but be ye transformed by the renewing of your mind, that ye may prove that good, and acceptable and perfect will of God.

Repent it, turn it, quit it should be the lasting motto of every believer. These words repent, turn and quit are expressive of the goals of salvation for every believer. They seal up what Jesus came to earth to do; restore, bring the restitution man needed to get back in right relationship with God once more and again. They describe God's principle of behavior.

To repent means we realize for sure that we did something wrong. We feel sorry or self-reproachful for what we have done or have not done that we are aware need to be done. We are conscience stricken or contrite often with feelings of regret or dissatisfaction over some past action or intention.

We realize further what we are doing that needs work to bring some improvement to our life. We know that a change of mind in some way must accompany our actions that we stop, quit doing that which we know is wrong. The righteous turns away from sin and stop doing them.

When a righteous man turns away from his righteousness and commits iniquity and dies in them; for his iniquity that he hath done shall he die, **Ezekiel 18:26**. We say to our soul that we have time, we have goods laid up for many years so I will enjoy myself now and consider to save you at a later time.

Many have left righteous living after Christ to return to the hog pin of life where they wallow in sin for a season that they may get caught up in hell for eternity. Eat, drink and be merry if you like but never forget about our soul that will live after we have called it a night to life.

We seek to differ, to be unlike the world. We are in the world but not of the world. God didn't take man from the world, the trees, the animals, stars, moon or sun. He took dust and water and formed a body and put man that He created in his image. Who we are is on the inside the body; the soul.

We must seek not to have our hearts overcharged with the cares and pleasures of this world. We must set our affections on the things of God that our soul lives. Who knows the spirit of man that goes upward better than he that gave it and the spirit of the beast that goes downward to the earth?

Solomon asked this question in *Ecclesiastes 3:21* because it was a time when man lived to be blessed and have great possessions. Ecclesiastes is an exceedingly human book. It faithfully mirrors the experiences of those who dwelled in the realm of material things. This shows how the little the world can satisfy the soul of man apart from God.

We too must hold fast to our God as Jesus before us did that our soul to be preserved for heaven. Fear not Jesus said in *Matthew 10:28* them which kill the body, but are not able to kill the soul; but rather fear him which is able to destroy both soul and body in hell. We are to fear God for the keeping of our soul; the principal of life.

Man obtained his higher spiritual nature, soul and personality that lives on after this life because it is a part of God's divine plan. James said in **James 1:21** that we are to lay aside all filthiness and superfluity of naughtiness and receive with meekness the engrafted Word, which is able to save your souls. Put away all worldly excess planted throughout our lives.

Peter in **1 Peter 1:9** said concerning us being an overcomer; receiving the end of your faith, even the salvation of your souls that we search to know that our soul is of utmost importance with God. We are kept through the power of God, through sanctification of the Spirit unto obedience and sprinkling of the blood of Jesus Christ.

Man's soul is an inheritance from God incorruptible and undefiled, it fades not away, reserved in heaven for us. Jesus asked the question in **Matthew 16:26** for what is a man profited if he shall gain the whole world and lose his own soul? Jesus declares the supreme value of man's soul. Save it alive! Save our souls alive today, live to live again!

THE BUILT UP SOUL

Turning Choices

Turning choices, what are choices and why do we have to make a turn with those choices? There is sin to the Spirit and sin to the flesh.

Genesis 3:5 For God doth know that in the day ye eat thereof, then your eyes shall be opened and ye shall be as gods, knowing good and evil.

James 4:17 Therefore, to him who *knows to do good* and does *not do* it, to him it is *sin*. Evil is birth forth in the heart. So then we *know* the *good* things that we should *do* and don't *do them*, we are in sin.

Man's humble beginning began when GOD CREATED AND, AND, AND, AND, AND HE MADE MAN AND WOMAN

Genesis 2:5-7, 18, 21-25, there was not a man to till the ground for man was yet in the spiritual state God had created him in. A midst from the earth watered the whole face of the ground. And the Lord God formed man of the dust of the ground and breathed into his nostrils the breath of life (His Spirit) and man became a living soul. And the Lord God said, it is not good that the man should be alone; I will make him an helpmeet for him (a helper fit just for him). And the Lord God caused a deep sleep to fall upon Adam and he slept and he took one of his ribs (God performed the first Caesarian section) and closed up the flesh instead thereof; and the rib which the Lord God had taken from man, made he a woman and brought her unto the man (no more male and female together in flesh; God took and birth her forth out of the made man).

THE BUILT UP SOUL

God is the Creator of man, animals, trees, things, rivers and the whole earth. Adam named the rib, which the Lord God had taken from him woman. This is now bone of my bones and flesh of my flesh, she shall be called woman because she was taken out of man!

At last, he too would have a mate as everything else in earth had to mate, be fruitful, reproduce and replenish the earth as God had already told them. God immediately married them in flesh to make them one with Him again in Spirit. Marriage is a covenant between God, man, and woman.

Therefore (God talking to the totality of man to come after these two) shall a man leave his father and his mother, and shall cleave unto his wife, and they shall be one flesh (note that oneness, let no man put asunder what God has joined together).

Marriage is God Ordained, Sacred. It should not be entered in lightly! Lock at how pure it was suppose to be; and they were both naked, the man and his wife, and were not ashamed. They were in the world but not of the world for they were like God; SPIRITUAL BEINGS!

When Adam was created in this world, he knew nothing of the world. He just roamed around in the world with Eve at his side free from the contaminants of the earth. God had made them in the earth but they knew not the world they were in. But thanks to the mean subtle demonic force; Satan they would soon like a new born baby learn some things about where they were.

They were sinless, full of light. There were no darkness in them for they were the light of the world. They were full of God. They set in a high place, a city that could not be hid for their purity illuminated the earth.

THE BUILT UP SOUL

The light of the body is the eye; therefore when thine eye is single Jesus said in **Luke 11:34** thy whole body also is full of light; but when thine eye is evil, thy body also is full of darkness. When we God's created and made beings realize who we really are; we too will choose light over darkness. It was in God we had life; its still like that today.

When life as we know it is passed; we still have life in the Spirit that man was in his first state. Adam and Eve were created first spiritually, then made naturally. God's light shined through them even after they were put inside made bodies; different in nature with different functions. Samuel said in **I Samuel 20:3** truly as the Lord liveth and as thy soul liveth, there is but one step between me and death.

Because of the spiritual death Adam and Eve brought forth to man, death now both naturally and spiritually happens. Death is imminent and we know not when it will come. We are in the world but not of the world. How death finds us and our life lived determines our resting place away from earth.

The light of God that shined forth within them was replaced with emptiness and darkness; yet they comprehended it not. They knew a change came because they found themselves naked as they always was. But something happened and they knew it; but didn't know until God spoke his disapproval of their actions.

God still tell man today of our sins. Repent them and quit doing them! We are better than what the world have to offer us! Be the light with the light God sent to bring man out of darkness once again! Hear one day God say welcome home thy good and faithful servant; enter into rest.

In the world man fight demons. Demons are evil spirits. Demons attack those that are obedient to

THE BUILT UP SOUL

God as well as those who are not. Satan has no respect of person; he want all of man to be afflicted in some area. Many are possessed with demons.

In the church man fights evil. Evil is misfortune developed by the mind and heart of one that know God, but fails to recognize the use of their mind, heart or body for wickedness. It means that before something is done that it has been pondering in the heart of the individual to actually commit the act.

There is a consciousness of the act gt times too late. Satan makes man to commit acts

Adam and Eve had no consciousness of the act they committed although they had been warned not to eat of the tree of good and evil. They walked around the Garden as spiritual beings in the Spirit as God is. They found the flesh seeking that which God had disallowed. They sinned a sin in the Spirit!

Their eyes came open to good and evil as God had said, but it also birth forth demons in the process. To them that has been taught the way, been taught to do good and do it not; it is sin, We birth forth satanic demonic evil spirits to attack.

Satan, as God does uses our mouth, eyes, hands, feet, heart, and mind to bring his attack against man in the earth. He first used a serpent to get to (beguile) Eve, to make her talk back to say what God had said that he could plant doubt. He copies off of God and keep God's order that man be deceived. He so make it seem like or look like God. He is a subtle evil foe..

So then, anyone who knows the right thing to do and fails to do it is committing a sin. Remember, it is sin to know what you ought to do and then not do it. Anyone, then, who knows the right thing to do and fails to do it, commits sin.

Whoever knows what is right to do and fails to do it, for him it is sin because Jesus' death burial, and resurrection brought back a choice to man to do right and turn from evil.

According to Paul in *2 Thessalonians 2:7-12* man will be condemned that chooses to walk away from God to follow after Satan. John in *Revelation 13:4* describes them as those who worshipped the dragon, which gave power unto the beast. He seeks to steal God's glory.

As with Satan they would be deceived through the mystery of iniquity that works in them because they keep not the law of God. One day the wicked one will be revealed and the Lord shall consume him with the spirit of his mouth and destroy with the brightness of his coming.

Satan will be destroyed, slayed, killed as well as those that come after the working of Satan with all power, signs and wonders; with all deceivableness of unrighteousness in them that perish, because they received not the love of the truth, that they might be saved.

For this cause God will send them a strong delusion that they should believe a lie; that they might be damned who believe not the truth but had pleasure in unrighteousness; the error of their way.

We have a turning choice that we don't be in the earth deceived by the means of the miracles which Satan have power to do in the sight of sinful men.

THE BUILT UP SOUL

He will have man making images to him by the falseness and lying of his way. Man chooses to believe a lie than the truth.

Its time we make a turning choice not to serve Satan and sin that we might live unto Christ and have everlasting life, eternally in heaven with God.

Colossians 3:25 but he that doeth wrong shall receive for the wrong which he hath done; and there is no respect of persons. Adam, Eve and the serpent all suffered punishment not only for themselves but for all of mankind and snakes that came after them, Genesis

Church persecution comes in by way of the church mostly. When it comes from church folks it is considered evil because they have thought on the thing and flipped it over and over in their mind and it has traveled from their heart to commit the act.

1 Thessalonians 2:14-15 for ye brethren became followers of the churches of God which in Judaea are in Christ Jesus; for ye have suffered like things of your own countrymen, even as they have of the Jews. The Church of the world in Jesus time on earth persecuted him. We too today that walk upright before God will also be persecuted.

Persecution in the Church turns the sinner back to their old ways of sin. *James 5:19-20* says brethren if any of you do err from the truth and one convert him; let him know that he which converted the sinner from the error of his way, shall save a soul from death and shall hide a multitude of sin. We are to convert the sinner to Christ.

THE BUILT UP SOUL

We Have An Inherited Blessing

We have an inheritance that calls for obedience to God. From the beginning man was told to obey. This neglect by man to obey caused man to be stripped of the inheritance God had for them. They lost their spiritual state, covering and inheritance.

Genesis 3:7-8 and the eyes of them both were opened and they knew that they were naked, and they sold fig leaves together and made themselves aprons. And they heard the voice of the Lord God walking in the garden in the cool of the day: and Adam and his wife hid themselves from the presence of the Lord God amongst the trees of the garden.

When Issac was 60 years old his wife Rebekah bore him twins, Esau and Jacob. Esau was first, so Jacob was born second. Issac loved his sons but was more partial to Esau while Rebekah favored Jacob. Positive deception and fraud would follow her misguided feelings.

Genesis 27:34-36 and when Esau heard the words of his father he cried with a great and exceeding bitter cry, and said unto his father bless me, even me also, oh my father. And he said, thy brother came with subtlety, and has taken away thy blessing. And he said, is not he rightly named Jacob? For he has supplanted me these two times: he took away my birthright and behold, now he hath taken away my blessing. And he said has thou not reserved a blessing for me?

Esau was the firstborn son of Isaac and Rebekah. He had been named Esau that means hairy because at birth he was all over like a hairy garment (*Genesis 25:21-26*). Because he was born first he would be promised the birthright inheritance of blessings.

As he grew older, he became a skillful hunter and frequently brought venison home to his father. On one very important occasion he returned home from a hunting trip famished, and asked for some red pottage (stew) that Jacob had just prepared.

Jacob requested Esau's birthright as payment, to which Esau consented surrendering the privilege of his birthright to Jacob rather than wait for the preparation of the food. He was going to eat anyway! Why would he give up so much for so little? *Hebrews 12:16-17* Esau sold his soul for a piece of meat.

Adam had before Esau's time gave up the Ghost for a piece of fruit affecting every human being that came into the world after him. What are we selling our souls for? Esau nor Adam realized at the time exactly what they had done. They both gave up their inherited blessing. How that all of our actions affect all those we love directly or indirectly.

When he realized that he gave up the inherited blessing of God; what he had done, it was too late! He was rejected, he found no place of repentance, though he sought it carefully with tears, *Genesis 27:38* and Esau said to his father has thou but one blessing, my father? Bless me, even me also, O my father and Esau lifted up his voice and wept.

All he received of his father was words he did not want to hear; you shall live by the sword, you shall serve your brother, and it shall come to pass when thou shall have the dominion, that thou shall break his yoke from off thy neck.

Acts 5:1-11 Ananias was a Jew that tried to enhance his reputation by a show of liberality. They died right at the point of the lie they presented to the Holy Ghost. They sold their own property to present an offering to God and lied about the increase they had received from the proceeds.

He pretended to give the entire proceeds to the Church, whereupon Peter detected the deceit and its deliberate purpose. Who should be able to recognize a lie is Peter; for he himself was caught up in a lying spirit where he denied knowing Jesus three times just as Jesus had said he would in **St. John 13:38**; the cock shall not crow till thou has denied me thrice.

Peter then laid bare the sin to the guilty conscious of Ananias who dropped dead at the revelation Peter had that he lied to the Holy Ghost. He was shocked that Peter would recognize his deceit.

Then here come Sapphira with the same lie not knowing her husband had just dropped dead before her. She too dropped dead with her lying, deceptive spirit. Ananias and Sapphira too didn't realize until it was too late that they had missed their inherited blessing.

The world today is full of fraud and deception. Issac was about 137 years old and thought he was near death. His eyes had waxed dim so he decided it was time to pass the blessing of rule and leadership to his oldest son Esau. Rebekah heard Issac speaking this and she induced Jacob to disguise and pass himself off as Esau. Esau here

on learning of Jacob's attempt to deprive him
farther of the blessings recalled how cunningly
Jacob tricked him out of his birthright resolved to kill
him when their father died.

Rebekah heard Esau's threats and his her favorite
son away. She sent him for protection in a safe
haven to live with her brother Laban on the pretext
that he was looking for a wife. His deception would
catch up with him; he had to work seven years for
the wife he wanted but did not get.

Now after the first wife, he would do double time for
that same wife he wanted in the beginning. We
must be careful in our acts, for we will definitely
reap that which we sow.

We have an inherited blessing; what are we willing
to give up to receive our blessings? In Bible times
as we see, the firstborn son became the new head
of the family. That means he would be responsible
for providing for the other members of the
household.

Such responsibility entitled him to receive the land
and lay their claim to a double portion of other kinds
of property. This was a customary inheritance. Only
a father had the right and power to transfer the
birthright from the firstborn to another as in this
case with Esau and Jacob.

Salvation is the inherited blessing for all men; it is
to the believers; heirs of God! And joint heirs of
Christ Jesus. I commend you all to God and to the
Word of his grace, which is able to build you up and
to give you an inheritance among those who are
sanctified.

THE BUILT UP SOUL

God wants to open our eyes and turn us from
darkness to light, from the power of Satan unto God
that we may receive forgiveness of sins and
inheritance among them which are sanctified by
faith in Christ.

The Spirit itself bear witness with our Spirit, that we
are the children of God, and if children, then heirs,
heirs of God and joint heirs with Christ. If we suffer
with Christ we will be glorified together.

Look for our inherited blessings from God.

THE BUILT UP SOUL

What's Our Hang-up

2 Corinthians 5:17 therefore if any man be in Christ he is a new creature; old things are passed away, behold all things are become new.

Ephesians 5:6-7 let no man deceive you with vain words for because of these things cometh the wrath of God upon the children of disobedience. Be not ye therefore partakers with them. For ye were sometimes darkness, but now are ye light in the Lord, walk as children of light.

Some things we are not to touch. We are to have nothing to do with. Our participation in the empty things of unbelief cause us to be in disobedience and it brings God's wrath down upon us.

Matthew 24:4 Jesus said to take heed that no man deceive us. We must not get caught up in being hung up; suffering from that which is emotionally disturbing, neurotic, repressed, baffled, frustrated, and stymied.

Micah 6:1-3 hear what the Lord say, arise, contend for the faith, plainly he say to plead his cause. We want God to be well pleased that we fall not into his anger where he be against us.

God has controversy with us, because we have lowered our strong foundation in Christ. We have hang ups. We complain, complain, argue and complain. If man hurt us, what has God done us. Wherein have God wearied us that He testify against us or we Him?

If we have heard God and been taught the truth in Jesus, put off those things that gets us hung up.

211

THE BUILT UP SOUL

Put off concerning the former conversation the old man, which is corrupt according to the deceitful lusts and be renewed in the spirit of our mind. We must give up some things. Be made new.

We put on the new man, which in Christ is renewed daily. We are to be reconciled both unto God in one body by the cross that we abolish the flesh. For it is through Jesus and the Spirit we have access to God.

We are not to fit in everywhere, in everything or with everybody. We get hung up on circumstances, condition, situations and people. We are built upon the foundation of Christ. He is our cornerstone where we are jointly fit together with God. We were never to fit in this world, for we were not of the world.

We must put a difference between us and sin. We can't sin, we must hate sin now because God hates it. We are now therefore no more strangers and foreigners but fellow citizens with the Saints and of the household of God. That mean we are not to be addicted, committed to the world or be obsessed by the what's in the world.

When we are devoted to God we are loving, loyal, dedicated and consecrated; faithful. Our religious worship is freely given, privately within with a deep affection for God. We are devout; showing reverence to God in life and service. Our praise, worship and life is done out in earnest, sincerity, and heartfelt devotion.

We must earnestly contend for the faith of Christ, having a constant adherence to the Word of God. We can't be as the hypocrite that have a pretense

of piety, an unsupported claim as to what they
confess but not profess in their known lifestyle;
backing down rather than stand up for what we say
we love and believe. Jesus was willing and did die,
give his life for what He believed to save us from
the penalty of sin. He is the connecting gear we
need to shift from earth to heaven.

The work of the Father, the Son and the Holy Spirit
was somewhat different with the one power that
works in all. God spoke the Word, the Word
became activated by the Spirit and things got done.
Each waits on the other to perform their part. They
usurp no authority over the other, put one another
down or backbite the other.

God has made plain the effectual working of them
all that man may understand their need and
purpose for each working entity of the Godhead.
They have specialized differences that is perceived
or expressed between them that describes their
function in the life of man. God the Father, the Son,
the Holy Spirit.

God calls man to also be different, become different
or differentiated. That means we develop new
character and characteristics that expresses a
difference between us and our fellow man that walk
not as we do.

There should be a distinguishable difference in us
and the world. what's our hang-up with being
different?

To be different is good when that notable difference
is the determining point or factor that makes for a
distinct change or contrast. God said in his Word
that we are to come out from among them (men

that walk in and love sin) that walks contrary to his Word.

We are told to put a difference between clean and unclean, holy and unholy. How can two walk together except they agree, *Amos 3:3*.

There can only be a difference of opinions when it concerns something man has said; not God. God's Word is true; He is immutable; He change not. He left no room in his Word to draw an argument, dispute or quarrel. What God said then; He still say today.

There is nothing that will change the outlook of God; God sees one way, His! Its time the Church, us stop compromising God's Word for the world to be happy in their sin.

It's time to stop being hung up on things that don't edify. The wrong thing to do is drop our integrity in Christ to please man. When we don't have any integrity we don't possess a state of completeness. We must be broken in our will to do the Will of God. We must be whole and entire, not impaired by hang-ups that separate us from God.

We can only operate in the soundness of God, His Word and Spirit; they only are perfect. We are trying to reach that same perfection. Our hope is entirely and all together resting in the faith and hope of God.

We must be of sound moral principles, upright, honest and sincere. *Luke 3:13* exact no more than what's been appointed to us. Able men fear God, men of truth.

THE BUILT UP SOUL

Take care of God's business in our life with special attention and precision. Let us not speak wickedly with our mouth. Let us incline our ears to wisdom that we be found and weighed in an even balance that God may know our integrity; wherewith we shall be judged. We are to hold fast our righteousness that is found in Christ.

When we get rid of all that comes to get up hung-up in things not like God, incline Solomon said in **Proverbs 2:2, 5** incline thine ear unto wisdom and apply thine heart to understanding; then shall thou understand the fear of the Lord and fine the knowledge of God.

Never let mercy and truth forsake us; write them on the table of our heart that we find favor and good understanding in the sight of God and man **Proverbs 3:3-4.** To walk sure in the way of the Lord we must do it uprightly before Him that our integrity guide us.

Proverbs 11:5 the righteousness of the perfect shall direct his way. We don't want to be hung-up on Satan's hang-ups he has set for us along the way. We are God's delight so we deal truly with all men. There is a way which seem right to man, but the end thereof is the way of death. Now do we understand why we are to be different?

We are as diamonds, precious stones unequaled in hardness and luster, transparent and capable of taking an unusual polish.

We must be polished and groomed in the Word of God to be all that God desires and destined us to be. Be different, be the difference God need to obtain the glory out of our lives. God desires diligence of us in seeking Him. We must esteem him highly and live apart from sin that we choose him over logic. Logic set parameters that have hang-ups attached. It keep us constant; we develop a constant adherence to the Word. We learn to obey every word written as we strive after perfection.

The quality of being diligent, makes us constant, be able to have careful effort that helps us to persevere in this way as we cultivate Christian graces. It keeps our heart and soul panting after God as we fulfill our labor of love in God's vineyard.

It helps us speed away from the presence of sin, help us to follow every good work and guard against defilement. Diligence give the degree of attention or care needed to help us endure this race set before us that we seek to be found spotless.

Diligence rids us of unlawful business both naturally and spiritually. It makes a way of escape for us in any given situation that we make our calling sure. How can we continue to be hung-up in this world system of sin?

If God be God, choose to wholeheartedly, with painstaking effort to stand for what He says in his Word. Those things he has revealed to us, do and keep. Give our own self, self-examinations. Teach Christ, instruct children in the Way; abound in diligence.

Don't allow Satan to get us hung-up on the things God gave us dominion over. What's our hang-up? God preserves us from evil, leads us to assured hope and we are sure to reap God rewards of favor, prosperity and honor. Stay rooted in hope.

THE BUILT UP SOUL

Spiritual Warfare

Spiritual warfare was in existstence from the beginning with Adam the first man; yet he knew it not. He was in the world but not of the world, for he had come from God. He only knew what God had given him dominion over that now existed in this world. All Adam knew was God. Eve was beside him and He brought her with him to meet God in the cool of the day to get the Word.

The Word is our weapon against Satan. When trials and testing come we better say the Word and know it! For the weapons of our warfare are not carnal, but mighty through God to the pulling down of strongholds, **2 Corinthians 10:4**. Satan tries to tie man up spiritually.

He didn't steal flesh from Adam, he stole his spiritual nature or state from him; that part of man that was in the image and likeness of God! Man eyes came open when they did the one thing God said don't do; touch not, taste not, handle not. Imagine that, all those trees in the garden and God said not to touch just one!

We today still seek hard for, look for, and lust after what has been forbidden us by God. There is the lust of the eyes, the lusts of the flesh and the pride of life that separates man from God still today in our time. We are to have no part of sin; run, run, run! Run to where?

Run to God, run to the Word of God, run to Jesus Christ; find God and keep Him real close. Seek for the Holy Spirit, the giver and keeper of man's life for the sake of the Father. Satan lied to Eve to deceive Adam, for Satan knew God, he knows the

THE BUILT UP SOUL

Order of God and is deceiving man still today to go against God's Order and orders. He planted doubt in Adam and Eve's minds to make them think God was the liar that he himself is; "did not God say you would truly die"; He knows in the day you eat the fruit of that tree that you will be gods like him. That's why he don't want you to eat; surely you want die.

They were already like God in their created state. They did die a spiritual death. Their eyes came open to the flesh after Adam ate the fruit at Eve's hand, Why? God birth forth Adam, Adam birth forth Eve. God birth forth the spiritual and Adam birth forth the natural.

God put man over the woman; he was the head of Eve. The dominion he had kept the Spirit in man alive. After he ate, it changed the course of man's life forever.

Jesus came to bring the Spirit of God back to man once again. The Spirit of God alive in us again gives God the rule. We receive his Word after we have heard it and apply it to our life. We now open our hearts to receive the Word and Spirit of God just as in the beginning.

The Spirit heard the Word; let us make man in our image and it was so. The Word and Spirit still work together to get the work of God done. Jesus came in the likeness of sinful flesh and showed us that when we obey God He works all things to our good.

He breathes his Spirit in man that we come alive in the Word. Then He allow the liveliness of His Spirit to infill us where we are Baptized in the Spirit. He gives man back what Satan stole from Adam and

THE BUILT UP SOUL

Eve but we have to work and do those things that God will be pleased with in our lives.

God never leave us alone to deal with the spiritual warfare we deal with in this earth. He gave us weapons through His Word and Spirit that if we follow we can obtain that once aborted spiritual nature back. Because Jesus came, defeated his and our worse enemy, Satan and put him under our feet we have hope.

Hope thou in Christ? Hope thou in God? Our hope should be in nothing less; for in the Creation, God was! The Word was! The Spirit was! It is in God we move, live and have our being. Take the Lord along with us daily; everywhere we go. He will in no wise turn us away; we turn away from Him.

Spiritual warfare is on every hand. When we go to do good; evil is ever present! But God! We must be mindful of that which goes further than we can see. We must study to show ourselves approved unto God and avoid the tricks and antics Satan tries to get us caught up in that we sell him our soul. He want to use our souls.

Now we need the Holy Spirit ruling in us that we see Jesus right and He lead us out of sin all the way to stand before His Heavenly Father. We need Christ now and he will lead us to the Father to be judged according to the Word of God! We need all of who God is to stand up against Satan. Jesus has given us the victory over sin!

Believe we need Him; God the Father, God the Son and God the Holy Spirit and He want to be all that to us. He will never leave us or forsake us; believe that! Don't be tricked out as Adam once was!!.

THE BUILT UP SOUL

Satan came to lie, steal and kill, but Jesus came that we might have life and have it more abundantly, **St. John 10:10**. He gives us the abundance in the Spirit to make us spiritually fit; its not in things we can touch, taste or feel.

Remember Adam and Eve had everything at their disposal because God gave all for them; all they had to do is obey what He had said. Too many seek after the natural things of life. Try now to seek after and find Jesus and let Him do the driving!

We need Him to move more than we can imagine or know. He gave us the ability to stand in the face of adversity; don't you want to follow Him to the end to see what it will be? He said in Matthew **24:12-13** that the love of many would wax cold, but he that endure to the end, the same shall be saved.

Don't delay come to him today that he can give us what we will need; all spiritual things to fight spiritual warfare!

THE BUILT UP SOUL

What Are We Feasting On

Do we know? Feast means festival, to eat an elaborate meal sumptuously, celebration, to honor God, anything that gives pleasure because of its abundance, richness or special treat. In Christ we delight in the Word, prayer and fasting. We delight in giving glory to Him. We keep Holy all that he commands us.

Isaiah 1:14-18 your new moons and your appointed feasts my soul hateth; they are a trouble unto me; I am weary to bear them and when you spread forth your hands, I will hide my eyes from you; yea, when ye make many prayers, I will not hear; your hands are full of blood. Wash you, make you clean; put away the evil of your doings from before mine eyes, cease to do evil; learn to do well; seek Judgment, relieve the oppressed, judge the fatherless, plead for the widow. Come now and let us reason together said the Lord; though your sins be as scarlet, they shall be white as snow, though they be red like crimson, they shall be as wool.

Lamentations 2:6-8, and he (God) has violently taken away his Tabernacle as if it were of a garden; he hath destroyed his places of the assembly; the Lord has caused the solemn feasts and Sabbaths to be forgotten in Zion and hath despised in the indignation of his anger the King and the Priests. The Lord has cast off his altar, He has abhorred his sanctuary, he hath given up into the hand of the enemy the walls of her palaces; they have made a noise in the house of the Lord as in the day of a solemn feast. The Lord has purposed to destroy the Wall of the daughter of Zion. He hath stretched out a line, he hath not withdrawn his hand from destroying; therefore he made the rampart and the wall to lament; they languished together.

Jeremiah laments the misery of Jerusalem and speaks of the actualities of Jerusalem's afflictions and their adversaries. The City's destruction is emphasized as a divine judgment upon sin. We just as Jerusalem must learn some hard lessons from God's Judgment.

Their sufferings as ours lead or should lead us to cast our self upon God's divine mercy. We need a new hope that God be again gracious to us when we purify ourselves away from the world's feast of Churches and back into the fold of God.

It is God's confession of his judgment upon his people because He is a righteous Lord and they rebelled against his righteousness, his Commandments and have gone into captivity, even the very young men and the virgins

God is calling for those that say they love him to act and live as He says they are to live; in strictness, Holy as He is. The priests and elders gave up the Holy Ghost to follow the way of the world. So it is today. Man use

natural feasts for a spiritual release to their
souls.

Because Lamentations deals with suffering as
judgment upon sin, the afflicted believer has
found in it the language of his confession, self
humiliation and invocation. They cry out to God
in their distress, their bowels are troubled, their
hearts are turned within them because of
rebelliousness and all around us is death.

Man's feast exclude God and they have no one
to comfort them. All of our enemies have heard
our trouble. God yet sees our wickedness and
our transgressions are ever before Him. God
had covered man's spiritual nature where they
knew not the flesh. They follow after their own
righteousness!

God is a radical God when it comes to feasts of
men, sin, and self-righteousness. We pollute all
that belongs to God in earth. God has cut us
off in his fierce anger. He no longer reaches
out help to us until we repent and quit our
ways. God becomes the enemy of the
disobedient.

He swallow up our blessings and allow
strongholds to over take us. We must change
us to be like God! It was we that walked away
from the Lord. We must make speed to hasten
to do God's Will, for his Purpose, His Way.

We must put away everything not like God that
His house is established in us. If we be willing

and obedient we will eat the good of the land while we yet hold the profession of our faith. Bit now if we refuse and rebel we will be devoured by the sword; destroyed.

Learn of God, do well, seek the feast of the Lord. Put away sin, God is looking and saying that even our solemn assemblies is as iniquity. Man does everything in God's house. There are feasts of flesh rather than feasts of righteousness. No soundness among men can be found.

The Prophet Isaiah warned of man's feast. He warned men then and us today that our rebelliousness will be confronted with judgment and grace. We today live in like fashion as the people of God did in Isaiah's time.

Isaiah was known as the evangelical prophet of his day. He gives the fullest and clearest exposition of the Gospel of Jesus Christ found in the Old Testament. Special emphasis is given to the doctrine of God; in his omnipotence, his omniscience and his redemptive love.

He reveals God as the one true God, the sovereign Creator of the universe. His master plan will be fulfilled in our life. He demonstrates the authority and inspiration of God's Word. Isaiah was moved by the Spirit. He makes known to us that God requires above and beyond the formalities of sacrificial worship; He requires of us to live a godly life.

THE BUILT UP SOUL

To this end he brings the most powerful
sanctions to bear upon the consciences of his
people through prophetic warning and appeal,
and in the pressures of chastisement designed
to lead them to repentance.

Make a commitment. Make a renewed
commitment to be in the feast of the faithful
guarantor of his gracious promises to forgive
all them that is repentant by deliverance from
the power of the enemy and sin.

God will protect us from the power of our
enemy that enslaves us to sin. We can't save
our self!

Awake and put on the strength of God. Shake
thy self loose from the dust we were made
from.

Seek the Lord while he may be found, call
upon him while he is near, let the wicked
forsake his way and the unrighteous man his
thoughts and let him return unto the Lord, and
he will have mercy upon him, and to our God,
for he will abundant pardon.

The happiness we seek is in God always; for
his thoughts are not our thoughts; nor his ways
our ways. Heaven is higher than the earth and
God's Ways are higher than ours; so seek his
feasts to fill our hearts.

THE BUILT UP SOUL

Bottom Line; God Is Always There

We need God, his Word and his Spirit. In the beginning God created the heaven and the earth, **Genesis 1:1**. In the beginning was the Word, the Word was with God and the Word was God, the same was in the beginning with God **John 1:1-2**. Bottom line, God is always there!

God the Father, the Son, and the Holy Ghost is in the beginning and is now today forever. We can't get around knowing Him. He is everything, everywhere, and sees all things. How can we escape so great salvation? Why would we want too; it testifies for us.

Deuteronomy 31:26 take this book of the law and put it in the side of the ark of the covenant of the Lord your God, that it may be there for a witness against thee.

Psalms 12:6 the words of the Lord are pure words, as silver tied in a furnace of earth, purified seven times. No matter what it is in earth, how many times we do a thing, the bottom line is; God is there. The law of God learned and followed converts the soul of man.

Hear what God speaks to us out of his Word for it is life, open our eyes that we see God as He is that we behold his wondrous law.

Psalms 10:14 we are helpers to the fatherless, those that know not God. God pitied us and we too must have pity on the lost as well that we as God has done with us, draw them into the fold of Christ.

THE BUILT UP SOUL

Psalms 68:5 God is the Father of us all; for without Him we are fatherless in the earth even if we have no natural earthly father present in our lives. David knew and declared unto us through God's Holy Word in *Psalms 89:26* that God was and God is my Father; My God!

Bottom line God is always there. God is divine; godlike, heavenly, and foretell. He gives us ordinances of divine service; Baptism, Communion, and feet washing. Jesus did all three when He was here. *2 Peter 1:4* reminds us that we are to be a part of God's divine nature.

How much is too much for God that gave and yet gives his all? Is it too much of Him to ask for our love? To know God is to love Him; to love him is to keep his Commandments, *Proverbs 6:20*. King Solomon said in *Proverbs 1:8* that we are to hear the instruction of our father naturally so; how much more God, the best Father of all? That's where his glory lie; within us.

We find God in his Word! We receive of Him through His Word. How we hear and perceive Him is important. We hear Him through his Word being read, studied and preached. We get our learning here in Church to take what we know to the streets. We are to win the lost at any cost; this is well pleasing to God.

Jesus trained disciples, taught in the Temple and then sent them to the streets to redeem the lost. Serve him up well. If we are not sharing Him with the world we not serving Him up well. It's harvest time; its time we too harvest souls. Show man that which is noted in the Scripture of truth.

THE BUILT UP SOUL

Our delight in God cause us to seek Him out daily that we meditate on Him day and night. David did find his delight in the law of God; His Word. He wanted to know what God would speak for he will speak peace unto his people.

The people that followed Jesus was also excitedly fed and said did not our hearts burn within us when we heard the Word, for the Scripture is being opened up to us, *Luke 24:32*. It pricks our understanding. Our hearts too should burn to hear the Word of God.

We should eat the Word daily just like we eat meat; for our spiritual life. *Isaiah 34:16* says we are to seek ye out of the book of the Lord and read. *Matthew 22:29* Jesus said ye do err, not knowing the Scriptures, nor the power of God.

Mark 13:31 Heaven and earth shall pass away, but my words shall not pass away. Bottom line God is always there. The Word keeps us; so then we should keep the Word, Jesus the Word lived in flesh said in *Luke 11:28* but he said, yea rather, blessed are they that hear the Word of God and keep it.

The Word is life, it will not depart us; we depart from the Word when we fail to obey it. God said in *Proverbs 22:6* train up a child in the way he should go; and when he is old, he will not depart from it. We leave the Word, He don't leave us. Bottom line, He is always there.

The Word keep us from walking perverse in the world that we be not a slave to sin. The spirit of man is the candle of the Lord; we must work to keep it burning. We must search out God to know what He requires of us and reach back to take someone with us. This journey is not for us alone. Mercy and truth preserved us; why shouldn't we want someone else to be preserved?

Life with us and around us is better with Christ for there lies our peace. The glory of young men is their strength, and the beauty of old men is the gray head. The blueness of a wound Solomon said cleanses away evil; so do stripes, the inward parts of the belly; *Proverbs 20:27-30*.

The Word is the living factor of God eternal in the heavens. Salvation is an inside job; for the Word must go on the inside to purge the evil that lurks within. *Isaiah 1:17* says we must learn to do well; seek judgment, relieve the oppressed, judge the fatherless, plead for the widow. We have work to do!

Bottom line is; God is always there to help us to accomplish his work. Come now and let us reason together, though our sins be as scarlet, they shall be white as snow; though they be red like crimson, they shall be as wool.

If ye be willing and obedient, ye shall eat the good of the land; but if you refuse and rebel, you shall be devoured with the sword; for the mouth of the Lord has spoken it.

From the time that we are born in the world somewhere we will hear the Word for the Word was already here. We must hold forth the Word of life. Let the Word dwell richly in all wisdom, teaching and admonishing one another in psalms and hymns and spiritual songs, singing with grace in our hearts unto the Lord.

THE BUILT UP SOUL

We make the Word work in our life. All Scripture is given by the inspiration of God. We take the Word and apply it in our everyday living

The Word comes as the Gospel, it is power for righteous living with the Holy Ghost being the keeper in us with much assurance. Our life now is sanctified by the Word of God and prayer. He is there to make us wise unto salvation through faith which is in Christ Jesus. We can taste the good Word of God and His power.

Through faith we understand the work of God through His Word. We know that the worlds were framed by the spoken Word of God. What we see may not be what we see at all. God of his own Will begat us James said in *James 1:18* with the Word of truth that we should be a kind of first fruits of his creatures.

We don't add to the Word or take away from the Word. If we do God shall take away his part out of the book of life he keeps on us. Bottom line, God is always there beholding the good and bad; He keeps a record on our life. What is written can keep us out of heaven; out of the Holy City. Now do you want to go? We must change us for heaven.

Hear the Word today, bare record of the Word of God and the testimony of Jesus Christ and all the things He saw. Keep those things that are written in the Word. Let the Word be true and every man a lie.

The Word of God is to us precept upon precept, line upon line and is able to keep us from falling. Its here a little, there a little that when we fall, He is able to pick us up again and send us on our way.

THE BUILT UP SOUL

The Word breaks down sin in our life that we be not snared and taken.

God sends his Word and we are to keep it, let it not depart out of our mouth, meditate on the Word day and night. Observe to do all that is written therein that we make our way prosperous and we have good success.

The Word, the Word of God, the Word of Christ, the Word of life, the Word of Truth comes calling right now to make a difference in our lives. He will be our sword cutting out everything in our lives not like God.

Seek the Lord while He may be found, call upon Him while he is near, let the wicked forsake his way and the unrighteous man his thoughts; and let him return unto the Lord and he will have mercy upon him and to our God, for he will abundantly pardon.

We need Him! Bottom line, God is Always there!

THE BUILT UP SOUL

A Mind Ready For Heaven

Colossians 3:1-4 since, then, you have been raised with Christ, set your hearts on things above, where Christ is seated at the right hand of God. Set your minds on things above, not on earthly things. For you died, and your life is now hidden with Christ in God. When Christ, who is your life, appears, then you also will appear with him in glory.

A new mindset encompasses not only a change in our mind and thinking but in all of our acts and actions. It causes a notable change to come into our life; in our talk, in our walk, and in how we pray.

If we were a liar before salvation a red flag should go up in our mind reminding us that thou shall not lie when we go to tell another lie after our heart has been pricked with the truth.

If we were a thief before salvation, we should get a red flag in our mind if we think about stealing again; for we are reminded that thou shall not steal.

If we didn't come to church before salvation regularly, after we are saved when Satan tells us we don't need to go; we should get a red flag up and hear the Spirit saying ***Hebrews 10:25,*** not forsaking the assembling of our selves together, as the manner of some is but exhorting one another and so much the more as you see the day approaching.

We are to not neglect God nor never stop encouraging one another. If we sin willfully after that we have received the knowledge of truth, there remains no more sacrifice of sin, ***Hebrews 10:26***. We have heard it said by renown men in the

THE BUILT UP SOUL

Gospel during our age that "once saved, always saved". Man according to their own mind and where they are in the sin of there lives will okay sin when its not against what they want to do. They will cause a nation to go to hell knowingly that their sin come not under scrutiny.

If after we are saved, Holy Ghost filled and Satan tells us that we don't need to give the church our money, tell him that God requires the tenth of the 100% He has blessed us with, We cannot actually afford to not brinf our tithes and offering to the altar God ordained and commanded we do.

Satan is a liar that knows God and His Holy Word. *Malachi 3:10* bring ye all the tithes into the storehouse, that there may be meat in mine house, and prove me now herewith, saith the Lord of hosts, if I will not open you the windows of heaven, and pour you out a blessing, that there shall not be room enough to receive it.

*Ephesians 6:1-*17 when we get a new mindset in Christ we not only think like Christ according to his Word but we put on the whole armor of God. Why? Put on the whole armor of God, that ye may be able to stand against the wiles of the devil, For we wrestle not against flesh and blood, but against principalities, against powers, against the rulers of the darkness of this world, against spiritual wickedness in high places.

Wherefore take unto you the whole armor of God, that ye may be able to withstand in the evil day in the evil day, and having done all, to stand. Stand therefore, having your loins girt about with truth, and having on the breastplate of righteousness; And your feet shod with the preparation of the gospel of peace; above all, taking the shield of faith, wherewith ye shall be able to quench all the fiery darts of the wicked. And take the helmet of salvation, and the sword of the Spirit, which is the word of God

Now along with that armor we have received with our new mind of Christ; a spirit of obedience. *Ephesians 6:5-6*. Servants, be obedient to them that are your masters according to the flesh, with fear and trembling, in singleness of your heart, as unto Christ; Not with eye service, as men pleasers; but as the servants of Christ, doing the will of God from the heart; With good will doing service, as to the Lord, and not to men: Knowing that whatsoever good thing any man doeth, the same shall he receive of the Lord, whether he be bond or free.

Our prayer life changes, *Ephesians 6:18-19* Praying always with all prayer and supplication in the Spirit, and watching thereunto with all perseverance and supplication for all sants; and for me, that utterance may be given unto me, that I may open my mouth boldly, to make known the mystery of the gospel.

With a new heavenly mindset comes a earnest desire to do God's Will. We speak those things that is of sound doctrine; our talk change. Its now all about God, not "I" or "me", or "you". Our lives transforms to be like Jesus.

Jesus sole purpose was to do the Will of his Father. When our mind is renewed after Christ we seek to also please God. We put our life on the back burner and allow God to have front and center. He lead and we follow. We want God to be glorified.

THE BUILT UP SOUL

We want to be found in submission to all of the Word; not just parts that we want to submit to according to our flesh. We don't serve God according to how we feel. Feelings have to be surrendered to the Word.

Being renewed in our mind means whatever it take to bring glory to God; we do it! God will comfort our hearts. Peace be to the brethren, and love with faith, from God the Father and the Lord Jesus Christ. *Hebrews 12:14* We follow peace with all men, holiness without which no man shall see the Lord. Without peace there is not holiness. God requires holiness in the life of man for it brings about peace that's found in the kingdom of God.

Romans 14:17 For the kingdom of God is not meat and drink; but righteousness, and peace, and joy in the Holy Ghost. When we seek for the Kingdom of God we must take on Kingdom mindset. Our lives will then encompass the true life of Jesus. One of love, peace, joy, and righteousness in the Holy Ghost!

God wants to bring heaven back to earth. This can only happen when we renew our mind to be like Jesus. Why Jesus? In the beginning was the Word, and the Word was with God, and the Word was God. The same was in the beginning with God. All things were made by him; and without him was not any thing made that was made.

In him was life; and the life was the light of men. And the light shined in darkness; and the darkness comprehended it not. That was the true Light, which lighted up every man that cometh into the world. Jesus was in the world, and the world was made by him, and the world knew him not. Adam

235

was also in the world but not of the world. He came unto his own, and his own received him not. But as many as received him, to them gave he power to become the sons of God even to them that believe on his name: Which were born, not of blood, nor of the will of the flesh, nor of the will of man, but of God.

We the people of God must have a mindset after the order of God which is opposite the one we were born with and taught of.

Paul said we have been raised with Christ, set our hearts on things above, where Christ is seated at the right hand of God. Set our minds he said on things above, not on earthly things. For you died, and your life is now hidden with Christ in God. When Christ, who is your life, appears, then you also will appear with him in glory, *Colossian 3:1–4*.

How can we develop a heavenly mindset? Some have said it is possible to be so heavenly minded that we are no earthly good. However, when we look at the history of the church, it was those who were the most heavenly minded who did the most good.

Listen to what Christ said in *Matthew 11:12*, from the days of John the Baptist until now, the kingdom of heaven has been forcefully advancing and forceful men lay hold of it. The people who forcefully grabbed hold of the kingdom mindset of heaven are the ones advancing the kingdom in earth.

Though we are in the earth, we need a heavenly mindset. Having a heavenly mindset is very important for advancing the kingdom, not only in our lives but in this earth as well. We are to call for the lost souls to Christ. How can we give men a Christ we never encountered? We must not only love Him, but know Him that we eagerly present Him to the lost souls in earth.

It is for this reason that Satan is always attacking the believer's mind with doubts, fears, worldly thoughts, and the likes thereof. Satan wants to keep Christians, believers from focusing on what really matters; God and his kingdom.

In the Lord's Prayer, we are taught to be consumed with God's name being hallowed, and his kingdom and his will being done on earth as it is in heaven according to Jesus in **Matthew 6:9–10**. The believer's mind should be consumed with heavenly things.

In Scripture, those who practice right thinking receive tremendous blessings. **Isaiah 26:3** says, "You will keep in perfect peace him whose mind is steadfast, because he trusts in you." It also can be translated, He will keep in perfect peace them whose mind is stayed on Him.

The person whose thoughts are consumed with God and his kingdom, will have perfect peace instead of anxiety and worry. When we find ourselves anxious or worried, we can be sure that we have lost the mindset God requires us to have to be about his business. .

Paul speaking in **Philippians 4:8–9** prays for unity and peace. Finally brethren, whatsoever things are true, whatsoever things are honest, whatsoever things are just, whatsoever things are pure, whatsoever things are lovely, whatsoever things

THE BUILT UP SOUL

are of a good report, if their be any virtue and if there be any praise; think on these things; those things we have learned or received or heard from God or seen in me, put it into practice. And the God of peace will be with you.

Paul says thinking on the things of God and practicing them brings the God of peace, the very presence of God into our lives. Many are missing the manifest presence of God in their lives because they have ungodly thinking, which eventually leads to ungodly acts and practices; the way a person thinks is an indication both of his salvation and his fruitfulness.

Those who live according to the sinful nature have their minds set on what that nature desires; but those who live in accordance with the Spirit have their minds set on what the Spirit desires. The mind of sinful man is death, but the mind controlled by the Spirit is life and peace, *Romans 8:5–6*.

The carnal person thinks only about the "desires" of his carnal nature. The carnal person may be spiritual, but he only wants things of the spirit that satisfy or glorify him:

God, give me, God get me into where I desire to go, God give me this job I want, God, take away this sickness from my body; every selfish thing we can think of; God do it for me. What about what God wants from us. A carnal person may believe in God and pray for things, but God is only a means to his desires.

James 4:3 says, when we ask, we do not receive what we ask for because we lack the faith needed

THE BUILT UP SOUL

because we ask amiss; ask with wrong motives that we may spend what we get on our pleasures.

However, a truly born-again person desires what the Spirit of God desires. He ultimately wants God's will to be done on earth as it is in heaven. This doesn't mean that we don't pray for our desires; it means we are not consumed with our desires. The desires of the redeemed should be and must become that of the Spirit of God.

Paul says the one who continually thinks on the desires of their sinful nature will bring forth the fruits of death and destruction, but the one consumed with the things of the Spirit brings the fruit of life and peace **Romans 8:6**.

The mind is very, very important. What does our mind say about us? It will tell us who we are; a believer or an unbeliever, a person led by the sinful nature or a person led by the Spirit. It will also tell us what type of fruit we will produce. A person that thinks on the things of God receives life and peace.

Paul says believers can develop a heavenly mindset by understanding their resurrected position in Christ. When Christ died, we died with him, and when he resurrected and went to heaven, we went with him.

Paul, in talking about the power that is in believers and was at work in Christ in the resurrection, says this power seated Christ in heavenly realms far above all authority, power, and dominion. God placed all things under his feet. If we are going to have a heavenly mindset, we must first start with understanding our position in Christ.

THE BUILT UP SOUL

Paul said we should not only seek things above but also turn away from earthly things. In order to think heavenly thoughts, we must get rid of or keep away from things that would draw us away from God. We are called to get rid of anxieties. Scripture says, "Be anxious for nothing" (**Philippians 4:6**). We are called to get rid of lust, anger, envy, jealousy, evil thinking and anything else that is not of God.

Practically, this may mean not watching certain TV shows, reading certain magazines or books, listening to certain music, or hanging around certain people, especially when we find they contribute to drawing us away from God and godly thoughts. We must zealously protect our minds. Paul said,

The weapons we fight with are not the weapons of the world. On the contrary, they have divine power to demolish strongholds. We demolish arguments and every pretension that sets itself up against the knowledge of God, and we take captive every thought to make it obedient to Christ (**2 Corinthians 10:4–5**).

We must take captive every thought and bring it into submission to Christ. Make no mistake here, brethren. Our thoughts are not neutral, innocent, or harmless. Our minds are either lorded by Christ or someone or something else. Is Christ Lord of your thoughts?

Again, our thinking is often affected by our friends. The fool in Scripture is a person who says there is no God or does not live for God, **Psalms 14:1**. Therefore, the wise are people who fear and honor God.

THE BUILT UP SOUL

At The End, Death

Jesus came that man be stripped for the Master's use. I must, you must, we must die individually to this world's goods. It takes a turning. We have been given new life. Death to this world and life with God must come naturally and spiritually.

Genesis 3:19 till thou return unto the ground; for out of it was thou taken; for dust thou art, and unto dust shall thou return.

Ecclesiastes 3:2, 20 a time to be born and a time to die. All go unto one place; all are of the dust and all turn to dust again.

I Corinthians 15:55-57 O death where is thy sting? O grave, where is thy victory? The sting of death is sin and the strength of sin is the law. But thanks be to God, which giveth us the victory through our Lord Jesus Christ.

We all (mankind) have an appointment with death! Is death something we give any amount of thought to? There is an appointed time that life as we know it in the flesh will end. Every one has a time to be born and a time to die. Do we wonder where we will go after our life is expired in earth.

At the end of the day; death, an appointment we all must keep! Man dread death and the old meaning of the word has been replaced with the softened phrase, "asleep in Jesus", for, He hath abolished death, **2 Timothy 1:10**.

Deuteronomy 30:19 life and death is set before us, blessings and cursing. Death can come by way of a lost blessed state in life. Sin prevailing in our life brings death to a righteous life. The choices we make in life is capable of birthing forth death in our lives. Death comes forth like a flower and is cut down, it flees as a shadow. A tree even when it is cut down may sprout up again. So it be with us, we die but will rise again. So then death in this life is not the end.

Job said in *Job 14:10* but man dieth and wasteth away, yea, man giveth up the ghost, and where is he? Job asked in *Job 14:14-15* if a man die, shall he live again? All the days of my appointed time will I wait till my change come. Job said man's hope is destroyed by some death that comes.

Death prevails against man and they pass. It changes man's countenance and sends him away. We all one day will go the way of death, from whence we will not return.

David said in *Psalms 23:4*, yea though I walk through the valley of the shadow of death; I will fear no evil, for thou are with me, thy rod and thy staff thou comfort me. Wise men like fools die too and even the brutish person perish. We all have an appointment with death.

David said in *Psalms 49:15* but God will redeem my soul from the power of the grave. Unto God the Lord belong the issues from death *Psalms 68:20*. Ye shall die like men and fall like one of the princes, *Psalms 82:7*.

Psalms 103:14-16 David remembered that we are dust. As for man, his days are as grass, as a flower of the field, so death flourishes. the wind passes over it and it is gone and the place thereof shall know it no more. After David had served his own generation by the Will of God, he fell on asleep and was laid into his fathers and saw corruption.

Psalms 104:29 thou hidest thy face, they are troubled; thou takest away their breath, they die and return to their dust. Man is like to vanity; his days are as a shadow that passes away.

Ecclesiastes 3:2, 19-21 a time to be born and a time to die. Man have but one breath, beasts have one breath, but death befalls them all. The difference between the death of man and beasts is the spirit of man goes upward to God and the spirit of the beast go downward to the earth.

Ecclesiastes 5:15 as a man comes forth from his mother's womb, he shall return. Naked man came and naked shall he return. He will carry nothing out of the earth.

Ecclesiastes 8:8 there is no man that hath power over the spirit to retain the spirit, neither hath he power in the day of death. Solomon said also a little farther in *Ecclesiastes 12:5, 7*, man goes to his long home and the mourners go about the streets; then shall the dust return to the earth as it was and the spirit shall return unto God who gave it.

Many preferably rather not discuss death but it is imminent. Isaiah in *Isaiah 25:8* said God would send his Son and his Son, Jesus would swallow up death in victory and God will wipe all tears from man faces. He farther said in *Isaiah 40:7* the grass withereth, the flower fadeth, because the Spirit of the Lord bloweth upon it, surely the people is as grass. Death dries things up. Jesus said he is the resurrection and the life, he that believe in him, though they were dead, yet shall they live, **John 11:25**. He said that he must work the works he was sent to do while he was alive because no man can work when night comes.

Night represents death but Jesus life. He is of God and God is not a God of the dead but the living. We therefore are to fear God that can kill the body and the soul. Jesus surrendered his soul in death to his Father, **Acts 7:60** and he kneeled down and cried with a loud voice, Lord, lay not this sin to their charge, and he fell asleep.

All men have an appointment with death one day. But on the other side of this death is the death of sin that will keep dying a death in Christ away from us all. It was by one man sin came into the world and death by sin, so death was passed on to all men.

For all have sinned and come short of the glory of God. Death has reigned from Adam to now. We shall though not all sleep but be changed. Death has been challenged by what Jesus did. We can be resurrected if we choose to be. It's a personal choice every man must make. For as in Adam all die, even so in Christ shall all be made alive.

Death is the last enemy to be destroyed. death where is thy sting? O grave, where is thy victory? The sting of death is sin and the strength of sin is the law. But thanks be to God, which giveth us the victory through our Lord Jesus Christ.

THE BUILT UP SOUL

From The Author.......

At Christ's second coming he will bring all things into full submission to his will. All will bow and call him Lord (*Phil. 2:10–11*). All things will be put under his feet.

The incredulous thing about Christ's rule is that we will rule with him. *Romans 8:17* says we are "co–heirs with Christ." Everything that is his is ours. In *John 17:22*, Christ said in his high priestly prayer that he has given us his glory.

Paul in *Colossians 3:1* is telling us that we must think about our resurrected position with Christ. Again he says: "Since, then, you have been raised with Christ, set your hearts on things above, where Christ is seated at the right hand of God."

Paul says our thinking should reflect our resurrection in Christ, the one who is seated at the right hand of God and will rule all things. In fact, Paul uses this same argument at Corinth where the believers were arguing and suing one another. Look at what he says: Do you not know that the saints will judge the world?

Do you not know that we will judge angels? How much more the things of this life! He essentially says, "Don't you know your resurrected position? Don't you know you will judge the world and angels?"

God has given judgment over to the Son (*John 5:22*), and because we are seated with him, we will judge the world and angels in his coming kingdom.

Why do men call God's people Jesus freaks? The Bible SAYS when we ask believing (It's according

THE BUILT UP SOUL

to our faith), be thankful (give God praise even though it has not manifested in the flesh yet) and wait on the promise.

Things may not happen as we want when we want; for whatever it was that we prayed and asked God for; we must know that God's got that for its in his hands. He have the power to do or not do for He is in control. Pray now and ask God for forgiveness for the anger we may have concerning the matter, nevertheless Lord not my will but thine Will be done in Jesus Name, Amen.

THANK Him everyday for all He put in our care, cover them with your blood Lord, and reunite us together for your glory, forgive all those that participated in our separation including myself Lord Jesus. Don't allow Satan to make us speak nothing other than this.

Satan is on his job to steal our joy, Rob us of our relationship by speaking doubt to our own prayer and eventually taking over our life that he can use us against God! Don't let him bound us I his web of deceit.

Death is God's business. we are to pray against every spirit not like him; that's our business where God is concerned so we must know how to recognize demonic spirits. Every thing that the devil stole, we are doing just as much for the kingdom. This is my Father's world, the earth and the fullness thereof. Satan has no days that is off limits; so we must work the works of Him that called us into his liberty that we be not deceived, dejected and denied.

246

THE BUILT UP SOUL

We are the true owners of this land and in all things we are to give GOD glory. We must hear his voice and do his bidding. "I AM REAPING THE HARVEST GOD PROMISED ME; TAKE BACK WHAT SATAN STOLE FROM ME- I REJOICE TODAY. I SHALL RECOVERY IT ALL".

We must make the corrections needed in our lives that we please God in our lives. The Scripture is written and it's right all by itself. They have already been tried. When we enter Satan's camp know that he is always pointing us to our gloom and doom away from the presence of God. We must be reminded that GOD keeps us where he sends us

it's always him teaching us. I was and am learning each and every day from Him concerning life. He make me, you, them, the others responsible for my or their own actions. He making us to be accountable for our own actions in life. HE is always making things real to man.

Keep walking and talking with your mind stayed on Jesus. Keep our hearts raised for praise. Let's stay sharpened for worship and delivered for God's use where He gets the Glory. Get up off the doubt and have faith to break down every stronghold Satan tried to bound us with. We are to use the weapons given us against spirits that tries to prevail against us. Keep a thanks in our spirit and on our lips!

The Do's And Don'ts Of Salvation

It is Christ Jesus that came in flesh to take life back from death. Adam was punished by God in Genesis 3: to face a death we were never to know.

Accept Christ

247

THE BUILT UP SOUL

Believe On Him

Confess Him

Deny Self

Explore The Word

Forgive Yourself And Others

Give God Your All

Handle The things of God With Care

Increase In Christ

Jump In Gear

Keep God's Commands

Love Like God Loves

Make The Adjustments

Need The More Of God

Open Up, Take The Overflow

Pray, Please God, Praise Him

Quit The Sin

Repent Daily

Stop Being in Today, Out Tomorrow

Use Christ As Our Godly Example

IT TAKES A TURNING

SAVE YOUR SOUL ALIVE

DON'T DROWN, TIE A KNOT AND HOLD ON TO GOD

REPENT IT, TURN IT, QUIT IT

THE RIGHTEOUS TURNS AWAY FROM SIN

WHEN A RIGHTEOUS MAN TURNS AWAY FROM HIS RIGHTEOUSNESS AND COMMITS INIQUITY AND DIES IN THEM; FOR HIS INIQUITY THAT HE HATH DONE SHALL HE DIE, EZEKIEL 18:26

CPSIA information can be obtained
at www.ICGtesting.com
Printed in the USA
LVOW08s0842210617
538808LV00001B/87/P

9 781543 428940